INSIGHTS

Into

Holy Passion Week

نظرة ثاقبة

لإسبوع الآلام

Insights Into Holy Passion Week

Designed & Published by:
St. Mary & St. Moses Abbey Press
101 S Vista Dr., Sandia, TX 78383
stmabbeypress.com

Library of Congress Control Number: 2018937305

INSIGHTS
INTO
HOLY PASSION WEEK

نظـرة ثاقبـة لإسـبوع الآلام

CONTENTS

INTRODUCTION

مقدمة

Insights into Holy Passion Week

The Passion of our Lord Jesus Christ expounded during Holy Week is a profound respective interval for contemplation, understanding, soul searching, repentance, and wholehearted gratitude for His immense love and the toll of His sacrifice for us. This special book provides deep insight and invites the believer to delve into an exceptional discourse regarding the events of the days and minutes of the Lord's Passion according to the readings and rites of the Church, starting with Hosanna Sunday, and unto Covenant Thursday, Great Friday, Bright Saturday, and Resurrection Sunday. Each day is comprised of significant deliberate details, prophecies, and personal messages, while engaging the reader to study the characters around the betrayal, the denial, the burial, the women bearing spices, the apostles, the guards, the religious establishment, and the pagan authorities. Christ's passion disclosed the disparity of truth

نظرة ثاقبة لإسبوع الآلام

تتبع آلام ربنا يسوع المسيح التى قاساها فى خلال الإسبوع الأخير، هو فرصة للتلامس الشخصى العميق معها، وللتأمل فيها، وفهمها، والبحث الروحى فيها، وللتوبة، ومن ثم نشعر بالإمتنان العميق عن حبه الكبير لنا ومعرفة مقدار التضحية التى قدمها لنا.

هذا الكتاب الخاص يقدم نظرة عميقة، يدعو بها المؤمن إلى الخوض في موضوع رائع يتناول أحداث الأيام بل والدقائق التى تألم فيها ربنا يسوع المسيح، وفقا لقراءات وطقوس الكنيسة، بدءاً من أحد الشعانين الى خميس العهد، ثم الجمعة العظيمة، فسبت النور، حتى نصل الى أحد القيامة. ستتابع فى كل يوم تفاصيل الأحداث الدقيقة التى مرت به، مشار إليها من نبوات العهد القديم، وستجد لك فيها الكثير من الرسائل الشخصية، مما يجعلك أيها القارئ المبارك تشترك فى دراسة الشخصيات التى تدور حولها أحداث الخيانة، النكران، الدفن، النساء

and love embattled with deceit and envy, and revealed the extent of the ultimate force of love compelling the Almighty, humble, and loving God to bow the heavens and lay down His life for the human race, the creation that He loves so dearly, to present us with the gift of salvation unto eternal life.

The accounts related in this book correspond with each day's events and should be read accordingly:

- Holy Week [Monday – Friday]: Before the First Hour
- Hosanna Sunday, Bright Saturday, and Resurrection Sunday: Before Matins

May the Lord fill all our days with the knowledge and passion of Christ, our Good Savior, to whom be all the glory, forever, Amen.

Bishop Youssef

Bishop, Coptic Orthodox Diocese of the Southern United States

حاملات الطيب، التلاميذ، الحراس، المؤسسة الدينية والسلطات الوثنية فى ذاك الزمان.

كشفت آلام السيد المسيح وميزت الصراع ما بين الصدق والحب وبين الخداع والغيرة، كما كشفت عن قوة الحب اللآنهائية التى غمرنا بها القدير الذى من خلال إتضاعه ومحبته طأطأ سماء السموات ونزل ليبذل حياته للبشر وللخليقة التى أحبها الى المنتهى، مقدماً لنا الخلاص كعطية مجانية غالية تقودنا الى الحياة الأبدية.

محتويات هذا الكتاب تتوافق مع أحداث كل يوم من أيام البصخة المقدسة، تقرأها الكنيسة بترتيب، فأحداث أحد الشعانين وعيد القيامة تُقرأ قبل البدء فى قراءات باكر من كل يوم، بالمثل فى سبت النور يتم قراءتها بعد الإنتهاء من صلاة التسبحة وقبل البدء فى صلوات باكر، بينما خلال باقى الأيام فى اسبوع الالآم فيتم قرائتها قبل الساعة الأولى من صباح كل يوم.

نطلب من ربنا ومخلصنا الصالح يسوع المسيح أن يعطينا أن ندرك آلامه المُحيية، له كل المجد إلى الأبد آمين.

أنبا يوسف

أسقف إيبارشية جنوبى الولايات المتحدة الأمريكية بالكنيسة القبطية الأرثوذكسية

Holy Hosanna Sunday

بيان عن أحد الشعانين

On Saturday, the ninth of Nisan in the year 5534 of creation, at the house of Simon the Leper, in the well-known village of Bethany (which means "house of misery" or "house of misfortune"[1]), Jesus Christ attended a dinner prepared for Him. Lazarus, whom Jesus raised from the dead, was also present. As mentioned by St. John the Evangelist, this is also when Mary [sister of Lazarus and Martha] anointed the feet of Jesus with pure, precious, fragrant oil, wiping them with the hair of her head: "Then, six days before the Passover, Jesus came to Bethany, where Lazarus was who had been dead, whom He had raised from the dead. There they made Him a supper; and Martha served, but Lazarus was one of those who sat at the table with Him. Then Mary took a pound of very costly oil of spikenard, anointed the feet of Jesus, and wiped His feet with her hair. And the house was filled with the fragrance of the oil" (Jn 12:1–3).[2] Six days before the feast was a Saturday.

حضر السيد المسيح العشاء الذي أُعِدَ له يوم السبت الواقع في التاسع من نيسان سنة ٥٥٣٤ للخليقة في القرية المعروفة ببيت عنيا ومعناه «بيت البؤس أو النحس»[١]، في بيت سمعان الأبرص، حيث كان لعازر الميت الذي أقامه يسوع من الاموات، وحيث دهنت مريم قدمي يسوع بالطيب الخالص الكثير الثمن ومسحتهما بشعر رأسها كما يقول يوحنا الإنجيلي «ثُمَّ قَبْلَ الْفِصْحِ بِسِتَّةِ أَيَّامٍ أَتَى يَسُوعُ إِلَى بَيْتِ عَنْيَا حَيْثُ كَانَ لِعَازَرُ الْمَيْتُ الَّذِي أَقَامَهُ مِنَ الأَمْوَاتِ. فَصَنَعُوا لَهُ هُنَاكَ عَشَاءً. وَكَانَتْ مَرْثَا تَخْدِمُ وَأَمَّا لِعَازَرُ فَكَانَ أَحَدَ الْمُتَّكِئِينَ مَعَهُ، فَأَخَذَتْ مَرْيَمُ مَناً مِنْ طِيبِ نَارِدِينٍ خَالِصٍ كَثِيرِ الثَّمَنِ وَدَهَنَتْ قَدَمَيْ يَسُوعَ وَمَسَحَتْ قَدَمَيْهِ بِشَعْرِهَا فَامْتَلأَ الْبَيْتُ مِنْ رَائِحَةِ الطِّيبِ»(يو١٢: ١-٣)[٢]، وبالطبع قبل الفصح بستة أيام يكون السبت.

The following day, Sunday, the tenth of Nisan, is the day on which every Israelite family would choose their Passover lamb from the flock, and keep it until the fourteenth of the month, when they would sacrifice it in the evening (Ex 12:1–36). On this day, Jesus entered Jerusalem publicly (Jn 12:12). Just as the Passover lamb is chosen and kept for a few days in the Holy City, likewise, the Lamb of God, who takes away the sin of the world (Jn 1:29), remained within the walls of Jerusalem, alternating between the temple and Bethany.

When the appointed time to fulfill redemption drew near, He entered Jerusalem in a great celebration, just as Zechariah prophesied concerning Him: "Rejoice greatly, O daughter of Zion! Shout, O daughter of Jerusalem! Behold, your King is coming to you; He is just and having salvation, lowly and riding on a donkey, a colt, the foal of a donkey" (Zech 9:9). Our Savior wanted to enter Jerusalem publicly at a time when pilgrims flooded the city to celebrate Passover. Josephus mentions that the crowd often totaled well over two million pilgrims.[3]

As Christ drew near to the city, they chanted with joy, such that their chanting reached up to the heavens. They chanted words specific to the awaited Messiah: "Hosanna to the Son of David! Blessed is He who comes in the name of the Lord! Hosanna in the highest! ... Blessed is the kingdom of our father David that comes in the name of the Lord! Hosanna in the highest... Blessed is the King who comes in the name of the Lord! Peace in heaven and glory in the highest" (Mt 21:9; Mk 11:10; Lk 19:38). Such words did not come from the people themselves, but rather, the people were moved to speak by an unusual force. They might not have understood the truth of what they exclaimed, but unlike previous occasions, Christ did not prevent the people in their praise because in this is the fulfillment of the prophecies. The Pharisees were livid and envious, and their hearts were full of hatred. Unsuccessful in their attempts to silence the people, the Pharisees asked the Master to rebuke the crowd, but He answered, "I tell you that if these should keep silent, the stones would immediately cry out" (Lk 19:40).

ثـم قـام في الغـد قاصـداً الدخـول الي أورشـليم علانيـة (يـو١٢: ١٢)، فـكان هـذا الغـد هـو الأحـد الموافـق ١٠ نيسـان، وهـو اليـوم الـذي كان يأخـذ فيـه كل جماعـة مـن بنـي إسرائيـل خـروف الفصـح مـن وسـط القطيـع ليحفظونـه الي اليـوم الرابـع عـشر مـن هـذا الشـهر، ثـم يذبحونـه في العشـية (خـر١٢: ١-٣٦). وكـما كانـت خـراف الفصـح تُفـرز وتُوضع تحـت الحفـظ بضعـة أيـام في المدينـة المقدسـة، هكـذا بقـي حمـل اللـه الـذي يَرفـع خطايـا العـالم (يـو١ : ٢٩) بـين جـدران أورشـليم مـترددًا بـين الهيـكل وبيـت عنيـا.

ولمـا قـرُبَ الوقـت المعـين لإتمـام الفـداء دخـل أورشـليم باحتفـال عظيـم كـما تنبـأ عنـه زكريـا قائـلاً «إِبْتَهِجِـي جِـدّاً يَـا ابْنَـةَ صِهْيَـوْنَ اهْتِفِـي يَـا بِنْـتَ أُورُشَـلِيمَ. هُـوَذَا مَلِـكُكِ يَـأْتِي إِلَيْـكِ. هُـوَ عَـادِلٌ وَمَنْصُـورٌ وَدِيـعٌ وَرَاكِـبٌ عَـلَى حِـمَارٍ وَعَـلَى جَحْـشٍ ابْـنِ أَتَـانٍ» (زك ٩ : ٩) إن مخلصنـا لـه المجـد أراد أن يدخـل أورشـليم علانيـة في الوقـت الـذي كانـت فيـه مزدحمـة بالزائريـن الذيـن كانـوا يقصدونهـا ليحتفلـوا بالفصـح فيهـا، وقـد ذكـر يوسـيفوس[٣] أن عـدد الجمـوع كان كثـيراً فـكان يفـوق المليونـين.

ولمـا قـرب المسـيح مـن المدينـة هتفـت أولـئـك الجماهـير بأصـوات التهليـل حتـي بلـغ هتافهـم عنـان السـماء، وهـم يشـيرون بهتافهـم الي الـرب يسـوع بعبـارات تخـص السـيد المسـيح المنتظـر «أوصنـا لإبـن داود، مبـارك الآتي بإسـم الـرب (مـت٢١: ٩)، «مباركـة هـي مملكـة أبينـا داود الآتيـة بإسـم الـرب، أوصنـا فى الأعـالى» (مـر١١ :١٠) مبـارك الملـك الآتي باسـم الـرب، سـلام في السـماء ومجـد في الأعـالي» (لـو ١٩ : ٣٨)، ولم يكـن هتـاف تلـك الجمـوع مـن تلقـاء أنفسـهم، بـل كانـوا مدفوعـين بقـوة غريبـة غـير عاديـة. لأن مـا فاهـوا بـه وإن لم يفهمـوه كان حقـاً، وقـد قبِلـهُ السـيد المسـيح ولم يحـرِّم عليهـم النطـق بـه كـما كان يفعـل قبـلاً في مناسـبات كثـيرة، لأن في هـذا كان كـمال النبـوات. وقـد حـاول الفريسـيون الذيـن أكلـت نـار الحسـد صدورهـم وغلـت مراجـل الحقـد في قلوبهـم، أن يسـكتوهم فلـم يفلحـوا، فقالـوا للسـيد إنتهرهـم، فقـال لهـم إن سـكت هـؤلاء صرخـت الحجـارة (لـو ١٩ : ٤٠).

Concerning our Savior's choice to ride a donkey that no one had ever ridden—as plainly written by the Evangelists that He rode the foal of a colt not trained to bear burdens—this is symbolic of Him as a new ruler of a new covenant who rode a new animal, and upon His death, He was placed in a new tomb. Since no one had previously ridden the colt, its mother accompanied it, symbolizing the Old Testament being fulfilled in the New Testament. This also corresponds with the milk cows from the Old Testament, which had never been yoked, that pulled the new cart on which was placed the ark of the Lord (1 Sam 6:10). Furthermore, riding a donkey was considered a sign of peace (our Lord Jesus Christ is the Prince of Peace), while riding a horse was a sign of war.

أما إختيار مخلصنا لأن يمتطي أتاناً لم يعلُه أحد، فقد نص عنه البشيرون صريحاً، ركب جحشاً إبن أتان غير متمرن علي الحمل، ولا ريب في أنه كان لهذا معني رمزي، فإنه كان رئيساً جديداً لعهد جديد، وإمتطي حيواناً جديداً، كما أنه عند موته قد وُضِعَ في قبر جديد. وذلك يطابق ما جاء في العهد القديم: أن البقرتين اللتين لم يعلهما نير جرَّتا العجلة الجديدة الموضوع عليها تابوت الرب (١صم ٦ : ١٠). فإن ركوب الحمير يُعد سلمياً (لأنه رئيس السلام)، بينما كان ركوب الخيل حربياً وذلك عند الملوك. وبما أن الجحش لم يركبه أحد قط، فيقتضى ذلك أن تصحبه أمه ليستأنس بها فيتمم هذه الخدمة، ليكمل العهد القديم بالجديد.

HOLY PASSION WEEK: MONDAY

بيان يوم الإثنين من البصخة المقدسة

Jesus Christ went out of Bethany (a city near the eastern foot of Mount Olivet, renowned as the city of Lazarus and his sisters Mary and Martha), an approximate two miles journey from Jerusalem—nearly forty-five minutes by foot (Jn 11:18), and headed for the temple. During this Holy Week, Jesus would spend His days in the temple, and return to Bethany in the evenings to spend the night. According to St. Luke the Evangelist, “In the daytime He was teaching in the temple, but at night He went out and stayed on the mountain called Olivet. Then early in the morning all the people came to Him in the temple to hear Him” (Lk 21:37–38). Traveling from Bethany to the temple on Monday morning, Christ cursed the fruitless fig tree, as recorded in the Gospel according to St. Matthew and St. Mark (Mt 21:18-19; Mk 11:20–21).

خرج يسوع من بيت عنيا الواقعة على سفح جبل الزيتون الشرقى التى إشتهرت بأنها وطن لعازر وأختيه مريم ومرثا، وهى على بعد خمس عشرة غلوة (يو١١: ١٨)، أى نحو ثلاثة أرباع الساعة من أورشليم قاصداً الهيكل، لأنه كما قلنا فى غير هذا الموضع كان يصرف هذا الإسبوع نهاره في الهيكل، وفى المساء كان يرجع الى بيت عنيا ليبيت هناك، حسب قول لوقا البشير «وكان فى النهار يعلم فى الهيكل وفى الليل يخرج ويبيت فى الجبل الذى يُدعى جبل الزيتون وكان كل الشعب يبكرون اليه فى الهيكل ليسمعوه» (لو ٢١ : ٣٧-٣٨)، وبينما هو مارٍ من بيت عنيا إلى الهيكل صباح يوم الاثنين، لعن شجرة التين غير المثمرة كما ورد في إنجيلى متى ومرقس (مت٢١: ١٨-١٩)، (مر١١: ٢٠-٢١).

Symbolism of the Tree

Christ cursed the fig tree because it only had leaves, and because normally fruits blossom along with the leaves.

ماترمز إليه الشجرة:

السبب الذى لأجله لعن السيد المسيح تلك الشجرة هو إنها كانت

The Gospel according to St. Mark mentions that it was not the season for figs to mature; therefore, there should not have been any leaves. However, although it was not the season for figs, in rare cases, some fruit trees matured ahead of others, and so, the presence of leaves on that tree was suggestive of an early crop, while in reality, the tree had neither unripe or ripe fruits, nor any sign that it would produce any fruits at all. The very leafy tree, barren of any potential fruit, was symbolic of the Jewish nation in its claim to be the sole holy nation on earth for its established law, the temple, the customs, and the religious rituals of fasting, feasts, and morning and evening sacrifices. Similar to the barren tree, it was void of faith, love, holiness, humility, and readiness to meet the Lord Christ and be steadfast to His orders. The Jewish nation boasted to be God's chosen people, yet rejected His Son whom He sent.

According to the prophets, the works of the Jewish nation spoke contrary to what they believed, as the Apostle Paul said, they "have a form of godliness but deny its power" (Cf. 2 Tim 3:5), therefore, the Savior pronounced woes upon them: "Woe to you, scribes and Pharisees, hypocrites! For you are like whitewashed tombs which indeed appear beautiful outwardly, but inside are full of dead men's bones and all uncleanness. Even so you also outwardly appear righteous to men, but inside you are full of hypocrisy and lawlessness" (Mt 23:27–28).

But, why look at the Jews, if we ourselves take on the appearance of piety, holiness, chastity, contentment, love, meekness, kindness, goodness, integrity, and keeping God's commandments, but do not fulfill any of these? Is this not also lying, hypocrisy, duplicity, conceitedness, and mental delusion? Does not every soul that sins crucify the Son of God once again? "And even now the ax is laid to the root of the trees. Therefore every tree which does not bear good fruit is cut down and thrown into the fire" (Mt 3:10). This is God's warning to all people in all ages and in all places throughout the universe of the woes of God falling upon them if they do not produce the fruits of holiness.

The Lord Christ cursed the fig tree, not because it did not bear fruit,

مورقة، والعادة أن يظهر الثمر مع الورق وينضج أحياناً بعض الثمر قبل غيره بأيام ليست بقليلة، وهو المعروف عند بعض العامة بالديفور. وجاء في إنجيل مرقس إنه لم يكن وقت نضج التين، وإذ لم يكن وقت التين كان يقتضى أن لا يكون فيها ورق، فوجود الورق قبل حينه فى تلك التينة كان كدعوي على أنها مثمرة قبل أوان الإثمار، بينما لم يوجد فيها شيء من الثمر الفج ولا من الثمر الناضج ولا أمارة على انها ستثمر. فتلك الشجرة الكثيرة الورق الخالية من الثمر المبكر والمتأخر، كانت تمثل حالة الامة اليهودية التى إدَّعت إنها الأمة المنفردة بالقداسة على الأرض، لأنه كان لها الشريعة والهيكل والرسوم والشعائر الدينيه من الأصوام والأعياد والذبائح الصباحية والمسائية، ومع ذلك فإنها خلت من الإيمان والمحبة والقداسة والتواضع والإستعداد لقبول السيد المسيح وإطاعة أوامره. فافتخرت بكونها شعب الله الخاص بينما رفضت إبنه الذى أرسله.

فبحسب نبوات الانبياء، أنهم بأعمالهم هذه كانوا يتكلمون بغير ما يبطنون، ولذلك واجههم المخلص له المجد بالويلات قائلاً "وَيْلٌ لَكُمْ أَيُّهَا الْكَتَبَةُ وَالْفَرِّيسِيُّونَ الْمُرَاؤُونَ لأَنَّكُمْ تُشْبِهُونَ قُبُوراً مُبَيَّضَةً تَظْهَرُ مِنْ خَارِجٍ جَمِيلَةً وَهِيَ مِنْ دَاخِلٍ مَمْلُوءَةٌ عِظَامَ أَمْوَاتٍ وَكُلَّ نَجَاسَةٍ. هَكَذَا أَنْتُمْ أَيْضاً: مِنْ خَارِجٍ تَظْهَرُونَ لِلنَّاسِ أَبْرَاراً وَلَكِنَّكُمْ مِنْ دَاخِلٍ مَشْحُونُونَ رِيَاءً وَإِثْماً" (مت ٢٣ : ٢٧-٢٨)، وقال الرسول "لهم صورة التقوى ولكنهم ينكرون قوتها" (٢ تى ٣ : ٥).

ومالنا واليهود، إذا نحن أيضاً تظاهرنا بالتقوي والقداسة والعفة والقناعة والمحبة والوداعة واللطف والإحسان والاستقامة وحفظ وصايا الله ولم نعمل ولا بواحدة منها. أليس هذا كذب ورياء ونفاق وغرور بالنفس وتضليل بالأذهان، أليس كل من يخطئ فهو يصلب لنفسه إبن الله مرة ثانية. "والآن قد وضعت الفأس على أصل الشجر. فكل شجرة لا تصنع ثمراً جيداً تقطع وتلقى في النار" (مت ٣ : ١٠)، فهذا هو إنذار من الله لكل الناس فى كل زمان ومكان فى جميع أنحاء المسكونة، بوقوع دينونة الله عليهم إن لم يأتوا بأثمار القداسة.

but because its deceptive leaves drew false claim to bearing fruit. God rebukes the unfruitful person in a similar manner in the Epistle of St. Jude: "They are clouds without water, carried about by the winds; late autumn trees without fruit, twice dead, pulled up by the roots; raging waves of the sea, foaming up their own shame; wandering stars for whom is reserved the blackness of darkness forever" (Jude 1:12–13).

Purifying the Temple

"Then Jesus went into the temple and began to drive out those who bought and sold in the temple, and overturned the tables of the money changers and the seats of those who sold doves. And He would not allow anyone to carry wares through the temple" (Mk 11:15-16). St. Mark arranged the daily events of Holy Week in chronological order. He mentions the events that unfolded on the first day that Jesus entered into Jerusalem; He "went into Jerusalem and into the temple. So when He had looked around at all things, as the hour was already late, He went out to Bethany" (Mk 11:11–14). So, as He was going from Bethany to the temple on Monday morning, He cursed the fruitless fig tree (Mt 21:18–19; Mk 11:20–21).

God also rebuked the Jews, in the days of Jeremiah the Prophet, for desecrating His house with idolatrous worship: "'Behold, you trust in lying words that cannot profit. Will you steal, murder, commit adultery, swear falsely, burn incense to Baal, and walk after other gods whom you do not know, and then come and stand before Me in this house which is called by My name, and say, "We are delivered to do all these abominations? Has this house, which is called by My name, become a den of thieves in your eyes? Behold, I, even I, have seen it,' says the Lord" (Jer 7:8–11).

To the Lord Christ, to whom is due all glory, the shouts of the buyers and sellers, along with the sounds of the livestock and their herdsmen in the temple, all seemed befitting of a den of thieves who were disputing while dividing the spoil, not as belonging to His Father's distinct sacred house. It is as though He was saying to them, "You are defiling my house by your unlawful commerce, because you stole God's right by turning the divine

لعـن السـيد المسـيح التينـة ليـس لأنها بـلا ثمـر بـل لكـثرة أوراقها، كأنها إدَّعـت الإثمار كذباً. هكـذا يعامـل اللـه الإنسـان الغـير المثمـر ويبكتـه بما جـاء فى رسـالة يهـوذا قائـلاً "غيـوم بـلا مـاء تحملهـا الريـاح أشـجار خريفيـة بـلا ثمـر ميتـة مضاعفـاً مقتلعـة، أمـواج بحـر هائجـة مزبـدة بخزيهـم، نجـوم تائهـة محفوظـة لهـا قتـام الظـلام إلى الابـد" (يـه ١ : ١٢ - ١٣).

تطهير الهيكل:

ولما دخـل يسـوع الهيـكل إبتـدأ يُخـرج الذيـن كانـوا يبيعـون ويشـترون فى الهيـكل وقلـب موائـد الصيارفـة وكراسى باعـة الحـمام. ولم يـدع أحـداً يجتـاز الهيـكل بمتـاع (مـر١١: ١٥-١٦). وقـد رتـب القديـس مرقـس حـوادث كل يـوم مـن الإسـبوع الأخـير بحسـب ترتيـب وقوعهـا، فيذكـر فى بشـارته أن السـيد المسـيح فى أول يـوم مـن دخولـه أورشـليم «فدخـل يسـوع أورشـليم والهيـكل ولما نظـر حولـه إلى كل شىء. إذ كان الوقـت قـد أمـسى خـرج إلى بيـت عنيـا مـع الإثنـى عـشر» (مـر١١:١١ - ١٤) هـذا مـن أحـداث يـوم الإثنـين. وأتى مـن بيـت عنيـا إلى أورشـليم صباحـاً وفى أثنـاء سـيره حـدث مـا كان مـن أمـر التينـة (مـت٢١: ١٨-١٩)، (مـر١١: ٢٠-٢١).

وقـد وبـخ اللـه اليهـود قديمـاً فى زمـان أرميـا النبـى عـلى تدنيسـهم بيتـه بالعبـادة الوثنيـة بهـذه العبـارة «هـا إنكـم متكلـون عـلى كلام الكـذب الـذى لا ينفـع. أتسرقـون وتقتلـون وتزنـون وتحلفـون كذبـاً وتبخـرون للبعـل، وتسـيرون وراء آلهـة أخـرى لم تعرفوهـا، ثـم تأتـون وتقفـون أمامـى فى هـذا البيـت الـذى دُعِـىَ باسـمي عليـه وتقولـون: قـد أُنقِذنـا. حتـى تعملـوا كل هـذه الرجاسـات؟ هـل صـار هـذا البيـت الـذي دُعِـىَ بإسـمي عليـه مغـارة لصـوص فى أعينكـم؟ هأنـذا أيضـاً قـد رأيـت يقـول الـرب» (إر٧ : ٨-١١).

وقـد أظهـر السـيد المسـيح لـه المجـد أن صراخ الباعـة والمشـترون، وأصـوات البهائـم ورعاتهـا فى الهيـكل، تليـق بمغـارة لصـوص يُقسـمون فيهـا المسروقـات بالخصـام، وليـس ببيـت أبيـه ومقدسـه الموقـر. فكأنـه يقـول لهـم دنسـتم بيتـى بتجارتكـم المحرمـة، وذلـك لأنكـم سـلبتم اللـه حقـه بجعلكـم المعبـد الإلهـى سـوقاً للكسـب البـشرى، وأضعتـم عـلى

temple into a marketplace for human gain, and wasted the worshippers' opportunity to lift up their hearts to God in prayer in His designated temple. You stole the money of strangers, raised the prices of items offered for sacrifices, and worked as money changers."

Teaching in the Temple

The Lord of glory spent this day in the temple; He drove out those who defiled it, not allowing anyone to carry wares into the temple (Mk 11:16), and taught and worked miracles. The chief priests and the temple guards were glaring at Him with anger, plotting His death, not yet able to carry out the evil in their hearts.

العباد الفرصة التي إغتنموها ليرفعوا قلوبهم إلى الله بالصلاة في مقدسه المعين لها، وسلبتم الغرباء أموالهم، وتغاليتم في بيع مواد التقدمة وصرف النقود.

تعليمه فى الهيكل:

وقد قضى السيد له المجد طيلة هذا النهار فى الهيكل يطرد المُدَنسين له حتى، إنه لم يَدع أحداً يجتاز الهيكل بمتاع (مر١١: ١٦)، وشغله بالتعليم وعمل المعجزات. وكان رؤساء الكهنة وحراس الهيكل فى ذلك الوقت ينظرون إليه بالغيظ ويتآمرون على قتله غير قادرين أن يتمموا ما تكنه صدورهم له من الشر.

HOLY PASSION WEEK: TUESDAY

بيان يوم الثلاثاء من البصخة المقدسة

The Master Teaches in the Temple: On Tuesday morning, the Lord Jesus Christ, to whom is due all glory, returned from Bethany to the city of Jerusalem. When His disciples were amazed (Mt 21:20; Mk 11:20-23), seeing that the fig tree which He had cursed had withered, He spoke to them about faith (Mk 11:24). Upon entering the temple that day, the Pharisees cunningly asked Jesus by what authority He does these things and who gave Him this authority. In His reply, He spoke of the baptism of John (Mt 21:23–27; Mk 11:27–33; Lk 20:1–8), the parable of the two sons (Mt 21:28–32), the parable of the evil vinedressers (Mt 21:33–46), and the parable of the king's son's wedding (Mt 22:1–14). The Pharisees then proceeded to challenge Him, and so, asked if it was right to pay taxes to Caesar (Mt 22:15–22), the Sadducees asked about resurrection, and the lawyer inquired about the first commandment (Mt 22:23–40). In return, Jesus asked the Pharisees about

تعليم المخلص فى الهيكل:

فلما رجع السيد المسيح -له المجد- من بيت عنيا في صباح يوم الثلاثاء إلى المدينة ورأى التلاميذ أن التينة التى لعنها قد يبست فتعجبوا (مت٢١ :٢٠)، (مر١١: ٢٠-٢٣)، فكلمهم عن الإيمان (مر١١: ٢٤)، وحينما دخل ربنا يسوع الهيكل سأله الفريسيون بمكر، بأى سلطان تفعل هذا ومن أعطاك هذا السلطان؟ فأجابهم على سؤالهم قائلا لهم عن معمودية يوحنا (مت ٢١: ٢٣-٢٧)، (مر١١ : ٢٧ -٣٣)، (لو٢٠ :١ -٨)، ثم ضرب لهم مثل الإبنين (مت٢١: ٢٨-٣٢)، ومثل الكرامين الأشرار (مت٢١ : ٣٣-٤٦)، ومثل عرس إبن الملك (مت٢٢ :١- ١٤)، وبعدئذ سأله الفريسيون عن جواز إعطاء الجزية لقيصر (مت ٢٢ :١٥-٢٢)، كما سأله الصدوقيون عن القيامة، كما سأله ناموسي عن الوصية العظمي (مت٢٢ : ٢٣-٤٠)، ثم سأل

their conviction of Him, and in so doing exposed their hypocrisy (Mt 22:41–46). He warned the people and the disciples of the hypocrisy of the lawyers and Pharisees (Mk 12:38–40), pronounced the woes on the scribes and Pharisees, and cried over Jerusalem (Mt 23:13–39). He then praised the poor widow who cast into the treasury the two mites, which were her whole livelihood (Mk 12:41–44).

When the Greeks asked to see Him, He spoke briefly to the multitudes, and then left the temple. While He was leaving, His disciples pointed out the magnificence and grandeur of the temple buildings, which led Him to reveal to them the prophecy concerning the destruction of the temple and their persecution by the Jews, and then, He cried over Jerusalem and her pending destruction (Jn 12:20–26; Mt 24:1–14).

When He went up to the Mount of Olives, He sat down and began to explain to Peter, James, John, and Andrew the chronological order of events and to take heed of the signs of His coming: the destruction of Jerusalem, the toppling of the Jewish nation and organization (Mt 24:15–44; Mk 13:1–23), and His Second Coming on Judgment Day. He also cautioned them to keep watch (Mt 24:45–51), teaching them from the parables of the ten virgins and of the ten talents—all this was on Mount Olivet (Mt 25:1–30).

When He had finished saying these things, He told His disciples that after two days would be the feast, and the Son of Man would be delivered up to be crucified (Mt 25:31–46). At the day's end, He went to Bethany to rest, and on this evening, the Jewish leaders plotted to kill Him (Mt 26:1–16).

The Temple

It might be a good idea to insert here a brief historic summary on the construction and subsequent destruction of the temple. Solomon built the first temple in 1005 BC "on the second day of the second month in the fourth year of his reign... at Jerusalem's] Mount Moriah, where the Lord had appeared to his father David, at the place that David had prepared on

السيد المسيح الفريسيون عن إعتقادهم فيه وأظهر لهم رياءهم (مت٢٢: ٤١-٤٦). ثم حذر الجموع وتلاميذه من خبث الكتبة والفريسيين(مر١٢ : ٣٨-٤٠). ثم أعطى الويل للكتبة والفريسيين ورثى أورشليم (مت٢٣ : ١٣-٣٩). ثم مدح الأرملة المسكينة التى ألقت فى الخزانة الفلسين وكانا كل ما تمتلك (مر١٢: ٤١-٤٤).

ثم طلب أُناس يونانيون أن يروه، وبعدها تكلم قليلا مع الجمع ثم ترك الهيكل، وفيما هو خارج منه أشار تلاميذه إلى فخامة وعظمة أبنية الهيكل، فأنبأهم بخرابه وإضطهاد اليهود لهم، إذ رثى أورشليم لأجل خرابها (يو١٢ :٢٠- ٢٦)، (مت٢٤: ١-١٤).

ولما صعد إلى جبل الزيتون جلس هناك وإبتدأ يشرح لبطرس ويعقوب ويوحنا واندراوس ترتيب الأحداث وعلامات مجيئه، وخراب أورشليم، ونهاية الامة اليهودية، وزوال نظامها (مت٢٤: ١٥-٤٤)، (مر١٣: ١-٢٣)، ومجيئه الأخير فى يوم الدينونة، والحث علي السهر (مت٢٤: ٤٥-٥١)، ومثل العشر عذارى، ومثل الوزنات، وكان ذلك على جبل الزيتون (مت٢٥: ١-٣٠).

ولما أكملَ يسوع هذه الأقوال كلها قال لتلاميذه إنه بعد يومين يكون الفصح وابن الانسان يُسَلَّم ليُصلب (مت٢٥: ٣١-٤٦)، ثم مضى إلى بيت عنيا ليستريح فيه، وفى هذا المساء تشاور رؤساء اليهود علي قتله (مت٢٦: ١-١٦).

بناء الهيكل:

ويحسُن بنا أن نُشير هنا في عجالة تاريخية الى بناء الهيكل وهدمه، وها هى: بنى «سليمان» الهيكل الأول سنة ١٠٠٥ قبل الميلاد فى اليوم الثاني من الشهر الثانى من السنة الرابعة لملكه فى أورشليم، فى «جبل المريا» حيث تراءى الرب لداود أبيه.

the threshing floor of Ornan the Jebusite" (2 Chr 3:2,1). There, he built a high wall, from the heart of the Valley of Jehoshaphat to the peak of the mountain, and filled the expanse between the dome and the wall with earth and stones.[4] Josephus the historian says that some of those stones were 45 feet high, six feet wide, and five feet deep,[5] and that the biggest stones were on the eastern side.[6] Solomon decorated all the rooms, floors, corridors, pillars, and gates that he built in the temple, overlaying them with gold and silver; one being of Corinthian brass.[7] Overall, "he decorated the house with precious stones for beauty (2 Chr 3:6). It took seven and half years to build (1 Kg 6:38), using in its construction 183,300 workers: 30,000 Jews (serving in rotations of 10,000 per month), and 153,300 Canaanites (70,000 carried stones, timber, and other materials, while 80,000 were sculptors and carpenters, plus the 3,300 overseers) (1 Kg 5:13–17).

The work was done at a remote construction site, "so that no hammer or chisel or any iron tool was heard in the temple while it was being built" (1 Kg 6:7). The front of the temple was eastward. Behind this was a slightly lower structure flanked by little houses that were entered from the outside.[8] Above them were houses overlaid with gold, which were exclusively reserved for the priests (1 Kg 6:8). Solomon's Temple stood for 424 years until it was destroyed by Nebuchadnezzar in 584 BC (2 Chr 36:6–7). Zerubbabel built the second temple (Ezra 3:2) on the same site of the first temple, 70 years after its destruction. It was inferior to the first temple in decoration and beauty: It did not have the Ark of the Covenant, which had been lost in the captivity, the cloud of glory did not appear in it, there were no Cherubim of glory, Urim or Thumim, or spirit of prophecy, and yet, it did exceed the first temple in glory and honor, because the Lord Christ had entered it (Hag 2:3,9).

Often, the kings of the nations who reigned over Jerusalem defiled this temple and vandalized parts of it. Herod the Great, however, renovated and repaired it to win the hearts of the Jews. He began this on the 18th year of his reign, in 20 BC. He employed in its renovation about 10,000 skilled builders. His successors continued repairing and remodeling it until

حيث هيأ مكاناً فى «بيدر ارنان اليبوسى» (٢أخ٣ :١-٢)، فأقام جدراناً عالية من بطن «وادى يهوشافاط» إلى قمة الجبل وملأ الفراغ الكائن بين القبة والجدران بالتراب والحجارة[٤]. وقال يوسيفوس المؤرخ انه كان طول بعض تلك الحجارة خمساً وأربعين قدماً، وعرضها ستةً أقدام، وسُمكها خمسة أقدام[٥]، وان أكبر حجارة فيه موضوعة في الجانب الشرقى[٦]. وزين «سليمان» كل ما بناه بالهيكل من غرف ودور وأروقة وأعمدة و أبواب، وكانت هذه جميلة مغشاة بالفضة والذهب وأحدها من النحاس الكرنتى[٧]. وبالإجمال فأنه كان قد رصع البيت بحجارة كريمة بهية الجمال (٢أخ٣ : ٦)، وإستمر بنائه مدة سبع سنوات ونصف (١مل٦ : ٣٨)، وقد إستخدم في عملية بنائه ١٨٣٣٠٠ شخصاً: منهم ٣٠٠٠٠ من اليهود وكانوا يخدمون بالدور ١٠٠٠٠ كل شهر، ومنهم ١٥٣٣٠٠ من الكنعانيين، فتعين منهم ٧٠٠٠٠ لحمل الحجارة والاخشاب وغيرها، و ٨٠٠٠٠ من النحاتين والنجارين، و ٣٣٠٠ ناظراً (١مل٥ : ١٣-١٧).

وكان العمل يتم علي بعد من مكان البناء «فلم يُسمَع فى البيت عند بنائه منحت ولا معول ولا أداة حديد» (١مل ٧:٦)، وقد كانت مقدمة الهيكل نحو الشرق، ومن خلفه بناء يقل عنه ارتفاعاً. وكان على جانبى هذا البناء غرف صغيرة يُدخَل إليها من الخارج[٨] ، وفوقها غرف مغشاة بالذهب لا يُسمح لإحد إلا للكهنة فقط أن يصعدوا إليها (١مل ٦: ٨). وكان قد بقى هيكل سليمان ٤٢٤ سنة الي أن هدمه نبوخذ ناصر سنة ٥٨٤ قبل الميلاد (٢أخ٣٦ : ٦- ٧). أما الهيكل الثانى (عز٣: ٢) فكان قد بناه زربابل مكان الهيكل الأول بعد سبعين سنة من هدمه، ولكنه لم يكن مثل الهيكل الأول فى الزينة والبهاء، ولم يكن فيه تابوت العهد اذ كان قد فُقدَ فى السبي، ولم تظهر فيه سحابة المجد، ولم يكن فيه كاروبا المجد، ولا الأوريم ولا التميم ولا روح النبوة، مع ذلك فأنه قد فاق الأول مجداً وكرامة لدخول السيد المسيح فيه(حج ٢: ٣،٩).

وكان كثيراً ما قد دنس هذا الهيكل ملوك الامم الذين إستولوا علي أورشليم وخربوا منه جانباً. وأخذ هيرودس الكبير يرممه ويصلحه ليستميل اليه قلوب اليهود. وإبتدأ بعمل ذلك فى السنة الثامنة عشر لملكه، وذلك كان قبل الميلاد بعشرين سنة،

the Jews' words to Christ were true: "It has taken forty-six years to build this temple" (Jn 2:20). The court of the temple was square, with each of its walls being 400 cubits.

Four Courts in that Temple

The **First** court was for the Gentiles and on its eastern side is the gate of the temple, which is called Beautiful (Acts 3:2,10). It is surrounded by porches and on the sides are houses, dwellings of the Levites. In one of those side houses was a synagogue or school for Jewish scholars. In that school sat Jesus when He was twelve years old, amid the scholars, listening to them and asking them questions (Lk 2:46). On those porches, Jesus spoke to the people. On them, the disciples gathered every day after His ascension (Acts 2:46). One of these porches gained more fame than others—Solomon's Porch (Acts 3:11). The height of this porch was 700 feet, and this is where the devil tempted Christ to throw Himself down from its peak (Mt 4:6). In that very court were tables for money changers and those who sold doves. It was called the court of the Gentiles because non-Jews were not allowed to venture beyond this point.[9] In Solomon's Temple, there were no court of the Gentiles; it only had the court of the priests and the great court (2 Chr 4:9).

Second was the court of the women; it was attributed to women not because it is especially for them, but because they are not permitted to venture beyond it inside the temple. They came here to offer their sacrifices.[10] Higher than the first court, it is ascended by nine steps.[11] The two courts were separated by a stone partition one cubit high, and a marble pillar near the steps on which was written a warning in both Greek and Latin to the Gentiles stating that anyone venturing inside would die (Eph 2:13–14).[12] St. Paul was accused of "bringing Greeks into the temple and defiling that holy place" (Cf. Acts 21:28). Jews engaged in regular worship in this court (Lk 18:10-14; Acts 21:26–30), and in its corners were 13 collection boxes for the worshipers to deposit their offerings (Mk 12:41).

وشغل فى ترميمه نحو عشرة آلاف من مهرة البنائين، وظل خلفاؤه يصلحونه، حتى صح قول اليهود للسيد المسيح أنه «بُنى فى ست وأربعين سنة « (يو٢: ٢٠)، وكانت فسحة الهيكل مربعة عرض كل من جدرانها أربعمائة ذراع.

وكان فى ذلك الهيكل أربع ديارات

الدار الاولى: «دار الأمم» وفي الجانب الشرقى من هذه الدار باب الهيكل الجميل (أع٣: ٢، ١٠)، ويحيط بها أروقه على جوانبها غرف لسكن اللاويين. فى أحد تلك الجوانب مجمع أو مدرسة لعلماء الهيكل، وفى تلك المدرسة جلس ربنا يسوع وهو إبن اثنتى عشرة سنة فى وسط المعلمين يسمعهم ويسألهم (لو٢: ٤٦)، وفى تلك الأروقة خاطب ربنا يسوع الشعب، وفيها كان يجتمع التلاميذ كل يوم بعد صعود الرب (أع٢: ٤٦)، وإشتهر أحد هذه الاروقة أكثر من غيره بنسبته الي رواق سليمان (أع٣: ١١)، وكان علو هذا الرواق سبعمائة قدم وهناك جرب الشيطان السيد المسيح بأن يطرح نفسه من سطحه الى أسفل (مت٤: ٦)، وكان فى تلك الدار موائد للصيارفة وباعة الحمام وأمثالهم. وسميت بدار الأمم لأنه لم يكن لغير اليهود أن يجاوزها الى الداخل[٩]. ولم يكن فى هيكل سليمان دار للامم فما كان فيه سوى دار للكهنة والدار العظيمة (٢أخ ٤: ٩).

الدار الثانية: «دار النساء» ونُسبت الى النساء لا لأنها مختصة بهن بل لأنه لم يسمح لهن أن يتعدينها الى داخل، فكن يأتين اليها فقط ليقدمن القرابين[١٠]. وهى أعلى من الدار الاولى فكانوا يصعدون اليها بتسع درجات[١١]، وفصلوا بين الدارين بجدار من حجر علّوه ذراع، وأقاموا قرب الدرجات عُمُداً من الرخام كتبوا عليها باليونانية واللاتينية إنذارات للأمم، خلاصتها أن من تجاوزها منهم الى الداخل يُقتل (أف٢: ١٣-١٤) [١٢]. وقد إتُهِمَ بولس الرسول إنه أدخل يونانيين الى الهيكل ودنس ذلك الموضع المقدس (إرجع الى أع٢١: ٢٨). وكان اليهود يمارسون العبادة العادية فى تلك الدار (لو١٨: ١٠-١٤)، (اع٢١: ٢٦-٣٠)، وكان فى جوانبها ثلاثة عشر صندوقاً يضع العابدون قرابينهم فيها (مر١٢: ٤١).

Third is the court of Israel, that is, the court for the men of Israel. The great court in Solomon's Temple included these three courts (2 Chr 4:9). This third court, higher than the court of the women, was ascended by 15 steps.[13] It was separated from it by a cubit high partition which had three gates.[14]

Fourth is the court of the priests, east of the court of Israel, where the altar of burnt offering and the laver lie. West of this court is the inner sanctuary, which is higher, ascended by 12 steps,[15] and before it was a court facing east which peaks at 190 feet. At its entrance are two pillars; one is called Jachin and the second Boaz (2 Chr 3:17), which divided the court into two sectors.[16] The first section is the Holy, which is 60 feet in length by 20 feet in width, containing the golden candlestick, the table of showbread, and the altar of incense (2 Chr 3:3; 4:19).[17] The second section is the Holy of Holies, a square, each side of which is 20 cubits (2 Chr 3:8). The partition between it and the Holy was a luxurious veil (Mt 27:51).[18] This temple was demolished during Titus' siege of Jerusalem after the Advent by 70 years, as predicted by the Lord of glory (Mt 24:2). Emperor Julian tried to rebuild it in 363 AD, but his efforts were in vain. He and the Jews were eager for its reconstruction. When they dug into the foundation, severe explosions occurred and fireballs appeared which destroyed the equipment, producing dust and smoke clouds to the point that the place became dark. In their second attempt, they were severely catapulted from the site, such that they abandoned all their equipment and their task despondently.

Romans Enter and Burn the Holy of Holies with Fire[19]

During the war between the Romans and the Jews, Titus ordered his companions and commanders from other nations to surround Jerusalem, besiege it,[20] and constrain the natives who remained, such that they would submit without having to enter into battle. When this was done, and the

االـدار الثالثـة: «دار إسرائيـل» أى دار ذكـور الإسرائيليـين، وكانـت الـدار العظيمـة فى هيـكل سـليمان تشـتمل عـلى هـذه الاقسـام الثلاثـة (٢أخ٤: ٩). بينـما كانـت دار إسرائيـل أرفـع مـن دار النسـاء، وكانـوا يصعـدون اليهـا بخمـس عـشرة درجـة[١٣]، وفصلـوا بينهـما بجـدار علـوه ذراع، فيـه ثلاثـة أبـواب.[١٤]

الـدار الرابعـة: «دار الكهنـة» وهــى شرقــى «دار إسرائيــل»، وفيهـا مذبـح المحرقـة والمرحضـة، ويوجـد غـربي هــذه الـدار الهيـكل الحقيقــى، وهــو أعـلى منهـا، وكانــوا يصعـدون إليـه باثنتـى عـشرة درجـة[١٥]، وكان قدامـه رواق متجـه إلى الـشرق علـو قمتـه مائـة وتسـعون قدمـاً، وفى مدخلـه عمـودان إسـم أحدهـما ياكـين والثـانى بوعـز (٢أخ ٣: ١٧)، وكان قـد قُسـم إلى قسـمين[١٦]، الاول «القـدس» وطولـه سـتون قدمـاً وعرضـه ثلاثـون قدمـاً وفيـه المنـارة الذهبيـة ومائـدة خبـز الوجـوه ومذبـح البخـور (٢أخ ٣: ٣، ٤: ١٩)[١٧]، والثـانى «قـدس الأقـداس» وهـو مربـع طـول كل مـن جوانبـه الاربعـة ثلاثـون قدمـاً (٢أخ ٣: ٨). وكان الفاصـل بينـه وبـين القـدس حجابـاً نفيسـاً (مـت٢٧: ٥١) [١٨]، وقـد هُـدِمَ هـذا الهيـكل في حصـار تيطـس لأورشـليم، بعـد الميـلاد بسـبعين سـنة، كـما تنبـأ عنـه السـيد لـه المجـد (مـت٢٤: ٢). إجتهـد الإمبراطـور يوليانـوس أن يعيـد بنـاؤه سـنة ٣٦٣ بعـد الميـلاد، فذهـب إجتهـاده هـو واليهـود باطـلاً، الذيـن كانـوا يطوقـون لإعـادة بنائـه، غـير أنـه لمـا حفـروا الاسـاس حدثـت إنفجـارات شـديدة وظهـرت كـرات ناريـة كـسرت أدوات الشـغل وثـار الغبـار والدخـان حتـى أظلـم المـكان ولمـا عـاود اليهـود العمـل فيـه ثانيـاً إندفعـوا بقـوة غـير عاديـة والقـوا جميـع أدواتهـم تاركـين الشـغل يائسـين.

دخول الروم إلي قدس الاقداس ذى العظمة والفخار وإحراقهم إياها بالنار[١٩]:

لمـا كانـت الحـرب قائمـة بـين الـروم واليهـود، أمـر تيطـس أصحابـه ومـن جـاء اليـه مـن الجمـوع مـن سـائر الامـم أن يحيطـوا بمدينـه أورشـليم[٢٠] ويحاصروهـا ويُضَيقـوا عـلى مـن بقـي مـن أهلهـا، فيخضعوهـم بـدون أن يتعرضـوا لمحاربتهـم، ففعلـوا كذلـك. فلـما طـال الحصـار عـلى اليهـود مـات أكـثر مـن تبقـى منهـم[٢١]، ثـم جـاء مـن هربـوا إلى تيطـس

siege dragged on, the number of Jews who died was greater than those who survived.[21] Some deserted to Titus, who pardoned them.[22] Then the Romans entered the city and into the House of God Almighty, reigned, and possessed it. There was no one to stop them; all the Jews feared the Romans.

Titus commanded his friends not to burn the temple.[23] Conversely, Roman leaders advised him that if he did not burn the temple, he would not be able to reign over the Jews or subjugate them, for as long as it remained, the fighting would not cease. However, if the temple was burned, the pride of the Jewish nation would also be destroyed and they would not have a reason to fight, for they would be brokenhearted and humiliated. Titus realized this, but still insisted not to burn it until he commanded.

The entrance into the temple had a great gate armored with silver plates. It was sealed because the Jews had locked it, yet some Romans came to this gate and smelt it to take its silver. While burning it, they found a way into the temple,[24] seized it, erected their idols, and offered sacrifices to Titus their Caesar. In lifting up their idols to praise him and accept him, they began to curse the temple and boast of Roman greatness. When the remaining Jews learned of this, they could not tolerate it, and a crowd of them went out by night to the Romans who had seized the temple and killed them.[25] When the news reached Titus, he went out with his soldiers to the temple and killed those Jews. The rest fled to Mount Zion and dwelt there.

The next day, the Romans gathered together and burned the gate to the Holy of Holies, which was fully overlaid with gold plates. When the gates fell, they gave out a great cry, which reached Titus, who came quickly to the Holy of Holies to stop them from burning it. He could not[26] deter them because, in addition to the Romans, many people including other nations were hostile toward the Jews and sought revenge on them. They ignored and overrode Titus, who was shouting at them loudly to stop. It was said that a group of his friends were killed on that day for entering the temple in great wrath, severe anger, and excessive rage. Titus had no control over

فقبلهم[٢٢]. ثم دخل الروم إلى المدينة وإلى بيت الله له المجد، فملكوه ولم يبقى من يمنعهم عنه، وأمّنوا جميع من كانوا يخافونه من اليهود.

وكان تيطس قد أوصى أصحابه وأكد عليهم ألا يحرقوا القدس[٢٣]، فقال له رؤساء الروم انك إذا لم تحرقه لا تستطيع أن تملك اليهود ولا أن تقهرهم لانهم لا يفتُرون ولا يكفون عن القتال لاجله ما دام باقياً، فاذا حرقته ذهب عزمهم و لم يبق لهم مايقاتلون عنه فتنكسر قلوبهم ويُذلون. فقال لهم تيطس قد علمت ذلك ولكن على كل حال لاتحرقوه حتى آمركم بحرقه.

وكان الطريق إلى القدس عليه باب عظيم مصفح بصفائح فضية، وكان مغلقاً لان اليهود كانوا قد أغلقوه بإحكام. فجاء بعض الروم الي هذا الباب وأحرقوه ليأخذوا الفضة التى عليه. فلما أحرقوه وجدوا سبيلهم إلى القدس[٢٤]، فدخلوا اليه وتوسطوه، ثم نصبوا أصناهم فيه، وقربوا ذبائحهم لتيطس سيدهم، ورفعوا أصنامهم بمدحه والثناء عليه، ثم أقبلوا يفترون على البيت ويتكلمون بالعظائم. فلما علم من بقى من اليهود ذلك لم يصبروا، فخرج قوم منهم فى الليل إلى الروم الذين فى القدس فقتلوهم[٢٥]، ولما بلغ الخبر إلى «تيطس» جاء بجنوده إلى القدس فقتل أولئك، بينما هرب من بقى منهم إلى جبل صهيون فأقاموا فيه.

إجتمع الروم فى اليوم التالى وأحرقوا باب قدس الاقداس وكانت كلها مغشاة بصفائح الذهب، فلما سقطت الأبواب صرخوا صراخاً عظيماً، فعلم «تيطس» بذلك فجاء مسرعاً إلى قدس الاقداس ليمنعهم من إحراقه فلم يتم له ذلك[٢٦] لأن الناس كثروا وإجتمع فيه خلق كثير من الروم وغيرهم من الامم التى كانت تُعادى اليهود وتطلب التشفى منهم، فغلبوا «تيطس» على رأيه وهو يصرخ بأعلى صوته ليمنعهم. وقيل أنه كان قد قَتَلَ فى ذلك اليوم جماعة من أصحابه، وذلك إنهم دخلوا إلى القدس بحنق عظيم وحدة شديدة وغيظ مفرط، فخرج الامر من يد تيطس ولم يقدر على منعهم[٢٧]. ويُقال أيضاً أنه صاح فى ذلك اليوم إلى أن بحَ صوته، ولم يُسمع كلامه.

the situation and could not stop them.[27] It was also said that in his attempt to command obedience, he lost his voice from all the shouting falling on deaf ears.

When he saw the splendor of the Holy of Holies and took in its magnificence, its serene beauty, and its abundant decoration, he was perplexed and amazed[28] saying that truly this majestic house should be a House of God, the God of heaven and earth, the dwelling of His Majesty, the abode for His light, and the Jews were justified in defending it and dying to preserve it. Nations were depleted, offering their best for this House, honoring it, offering it gifts and money. It is greater than the Roman temple and all the temples we have seen or heard of. God witnesses that this burning was not intended, but people did this out of their excessive evil and adamant nagging.

The fire caught in the temple and burned it up, and when the remaining priests received word of the entry of the Romans into the Holy of Holies, they desperately came to fight the Romans until they were drained. When they were overwhelmed from seeing the temple burnt, they said to themselves, "After the Holy of God has been burned, what reason is there to live and what life can we enjoy?" So, they threw themselves into the fire and were all burned.[29] The burning of the temple was on the tenth day of the fifth month, the same day in which the Chaldeans burned the first temple.[30]

When the Jews who remained in the city learned that the Holy of Holies had been burned, they went to all of the city's venerable mansions, palaces, and royal gates and burned them with all their many funds and treasures.

The day after the temple was burned, a man among the Jews prophesied saying that this House will be rebuilt without anyone rebuilding it, but by the power of God Almighty, so remain steadfast in your battle against the Romans and your resistance to obey them. When the Jews who remained heard his words, they gathered together and fought against the Romans,

ولما رأى قدس الاقداس وشاهد حُسنه وتَفَرس فى عظم بهجته ورائق جماله وكثرة زينته[٢٨]، تحير وتعجب وقال حقاً أن هذا البيت الجليل ينبغى أن يكون بيتاً لله إله السماء والارض ومسكن جلاله ومحل نوره، وأنه يحق لليهود أن يحاربوا عنه ويستقتلوا لاجله. وقد أصابت الامم وأحسنت إعظامها لهذا البيت واجلالها له، وحملها له الهدايا والأموال، وشهد قائلاً أنه أعظم من هياكل رومية ومن جميع الهياكل التى شاهدناها أوبلغنا خبرها، والشاهد علىَّ هو الله إنى لم أشأ إحراقه، ولكن القوم قد فعلوا ذلك من فرط شرهم وعظم الحاحهم.

ثم اشتعلت النار فى القدس وأحرقته جميعه، وإذ علم من بقى من الكهنه بدخول الروم إلى قدس الاقداس ليحرقوه، جاءوا مستقتلين، فحاربوا الروم إلى أن لم تبق لهم حيلة ولا قدرة على محاربتهم، فلما غُلِبوا علي أمرهم ورأوا أن البيت قد احترق، قالوا إن بعد احتراق قدس الله مالنا وللحياة، وأى عيش يطيب لنا بعد، فزجوا بأنفسهم فى النار فإحترقوا بأجمعهم[٢٩]، وكان حريق القدس في اليوم العاشر من الشهر الخامس. مثل اليوم الذى أحرق فيه الكلدانيون البيت الاول[٣٠].

ولما علم اليهود الذين تبقوا فى المدينة بأن قدس الاقداس قد إحترق مضوا إلى جميع ما فى المدينة من القصور الجليلة والمنازل الحسنة والابواب الملوكية فأحرقوها، مع جميع ما كان فيها من الذخائر الكثيرة العدد والاموال.

ولما كان غد اليوم الذى أُحرق فيه القدس، ظهر رجل بين اليهود يدَّعى النبوة قائلاً: إن هذا البيت يُبنى كما كان، من غير أن يبنيه إنسان لكنه يبنى بقدرة الله، فثابروا على ما أنتم عليه من مقاومة الروم والإمتناع عن إطاعتهم. ولما سمع كلامه من بقي من اليهود، إجتمعوا وقاتلوا الروم، فظفر الروم عليهم وقتلوهم عن آخرهم[٣١]، وقتلوا أيضاً جمعاً كبيراً من أمة اليهود ممن كانوا قبل ذلك قد رحموهم وأحسنوا اليهم.

but the Romans defeated them and killed all of them,[31] including a large crowd of the Jews whom they had previously pardoned and treated well.

Preceding Signs Indicating the Pending Destruction of Jerusalem[32]

Before the coming of Titus Vespasian, a great star with a very bright light sufficient to light up Jerusalem—luminous as daylight—appeared over Jerusalem. This lasted throughout the seven-day Passover holiday and then disappeared. To the general public and the simple folk, this star brought great joy, but to the scientists and the scholarly, it brought distress.

On the day of the feast, they had brought to Jerusalem a heifer to offer. When they came to sacrifice it, it gave birth to a sheep—leaving the people appalled and in denial of the event. The eastern gate to Jerusalem—a great heavy gate that required the effort of several men in order to open it, was found open daily on its own, so the simple folks rejoiced while the educated were disturbed. Next, the image of a very handsome, extremely gallant, and exceedingly luminous man appeared in the sky over Jerusalem. In the air in those days, there also appeared images of fiery riders on flaming horses flying close to the ground; this was seen in Jerusalem and in all the lands of the Jews.

Following all these events, on the eve of the feast of Pentecost, the priests heard the sound of many footsteps pacing back and forth in the temple, but saw no one. Then they heard a loud voice saying, "Come let us leave this place [the temple]."

Four years prior to the destruction of Jerusalem, an ordinary man appeared in the city, who walked among the people as a madman crying out loud saying, "A voice from the east, a voice from the west, a voice from the four winds, a voice against Jerusalem and the holy house, a voice against the bridegrooms and the brides, and a voice against this whole people!"[33] The people hated, rebuked, and were weary of him, imagining him a crazy fellow; this continued until the Romans surrounded the city. He was eventually stoned to death as he repeated his words in the midst of the

اشياء دلت على خراب القدس:[٣٢]

كان قبل مجئ «وسباسيانس» قد ظهر على القدس كوكب عظيم له نور قوى شديد، وكان القدس يضئ بذلك الكوكب كضوء النهار تقريباً. وإستمر ذلك مدة سبعة أيام عيد الفصح ثم غاب، ففرح به عامة الناس وجهلائهم، وإغتم العلماء وأهل الفضل والمعرفة.

وكانوا قد احضروا الى القدس فى ذلك العيد بقرة ليقربوا بها، فلما طرحوها ليذبحوها ولدت خروفاً، فأستشنعه الناس وإستنكروه. ومن ذلك أن باب القدس الشرقى كان باباً عظيماً ثقيلاً يحتاج لفتحه جماعة من الرجال، فلما كان فى تلك الايام كانوا يجدونه كل يوم مفتوحاً، فكان الجهال يفرحون بذلك وأهل العلم والمعرفة يغتمون له. ظهر بعد ذلك على بيت القدس فى الهواء صورة وجه إنسان شديد الحسن عظيم الجمال والبهاء ساطع النور والضياء. وظهر فى الجو أيضاً في تلك الأيام صور فرسان من نار على خيل من نار يطيرون فى الهواء قريباً من الأرض، وكان ذلك يُري على أورشليم وعلى جميع أرض اليهود.

وبعد ذلك سمع الكهنة فى القدس ليلة عيد العنصرة صوت جماعة كثيرة يذهبون ويجيئون ويمشون فى الهيكل من غير أن يروا أشخاصاً، وكانوا يسمعون صوتهم، ثم كانوا يسمعون صوتاً عظيماً يقول إمض بنا حتى نرحل من هذا البيت.

وقبل خراب القدس بأربع سنين، ظهر فى المدينة إنسان من العامة كان يمشى بين الناس كالمجنون، ويصيح بأعلى صوته قائلاً: «صوت فى المشرق، صوت في المغرب، صوت فى أربع جهات العالم، صوت على أورشليم، صوت على الهيكل، صوت على الحصن، صوت علي العروس، صوت على جميع الناس الذين بأورشليم»[٣٣]. وكان الناس يمقتونه وينتهرونه ويتصورونه مخبولا، ولم يكن هو يفتر من هذا، فلم يزل على ذلك حتى أحاط الروم بالمدينة. فلما كان فى بعض الأيام والحرب على المدينة

raging battle.

In those days also, an old stone was found on which was written, "That then should their city be taken, as well as their holy house, when once their temple should become four-square."[34] Thereafter, when Titus demolished the tower beside the temple, Antonia in Hebrew, the Jews rebuilt it and added it to the temple, such that it became square.

Although they had forgotten the writing on the stone, when they saw that the temple had become a square, they remembered. Thus, when they found on the side wall of the temple, a stone on which was written, "If the temple becomes a square structure, then a king will rule over Israel and will take over all the land," some said it would be the king of Israel, while the wise men and the scribes said it would be the king of Rome.

إبتـدأ أن يتكلـم بمـا كان يتكلـم بـه عـلى عادتـه فرُمِـىَ بحجـر عـلى هامتـه فـمات.

ووُجِـدَ حجـر قديـم فى ذلـك الزمـان مكتوبـاً عليـه إذا كمـل بنيـان القـدس وصـار مربعـاً عنـد ذلـك يَخـرُبْ[٣٤]. فلـما هـدم تيطـس البُنيـان الـذى كان بجانـب القـدس المسـمى بالعبرانيـه «أنطونيـا»، أعـاد اليهـود بنـاؤه، وأضافـوه إلى جملـة القـدس فصـارَ مربعـاً.

وكانـوا قـد نسـوا ذلـك المكتـوب الـذى وجـدوه عـلى الحجـر. فلـما رأوا القـدس وقـد تربـع تذكـروا ذلـك. ووجـدوا أيضـاً في جانـب حائـط قـدس الأقـداس حجـراً مكتـوب عليـه إذا صـار الهيـكل مربعـاً يملـك حينئـذ عـلي إسرائيـل ملـك ويسـتولى عـلي سـائر الارض، فقـال بعـض النـاس هـو ملـك اسرائيـل بينـما قـال الحكـماء والكتبـه بـل هـو ملـك الـروم.

HOLY PASSION WEEK: WEDNESDAY

بيان يوم الأربعاء من البصخة المقدسة

Our Lord of glory spent this day in Bethany teaching the disciples and assuring them that He would not abandon them. There is no mention in the Holy Bible that Jesus did anything on this day; He sought solitude and isolation from people on this day. He avoided the multitudes, just as the Passover lamb also rested before the day of its slaughter.

صرف مخلصنا له المجد هذا اليوم فى بيت عنيا فى تعليم تلاميذه، طمأنهم أنه لن يتخلى عنهم. لم يذكر الكتاب إنه عمل شيئاً فى هذا اليوم، ليشير على إنه -رب المجد- قصد الوحدة والإنفراد عن الناس وتجنب الإجتماعيات مثلما كان يستريح خروف الفصح قبل ذبحه فى اليوم المُعَدَ له.

Jesus Leaves the Temple

The Lord Christ left the temple on Tuesday evening and returned to Bethany with the intention of not returning to the temple ever again. This is why He told the Jews, "See! Your house is left to you desolate; for I say to you, you shall see Me no more till you say, 'Blessed is He who comes in the name of the Lord!'" (Mt 23:38–39). He is the true Lord of the temple, and had revealed this authority by telling those who sold doves, "'Take these things away! Do not make My Father's house a house of merchandise!' Then His disciples remembered that it was written, 'Zeal for Your house has

يسوع يترك الهيكل:

ترك السيد المسيح له المجد الهيكل عند مساء يوم الثلاثاء ورجع إلى بيت عنيا وفي نيته عدم العودة اليه البتة وذلك بعد أن قال لليهود «هوذا بيتكم يُترك لكم خراباً. لاني أقول لكم إنكم لا تروننى من الآن حتى تقولوا مبارك الآتى باسم الرب» (مت ٢٣: ٣٨-٣٩)، مع إنه هو الرب الحقيقى للهيكل. وقد بيَّن ذلك بسلطانه عليه قبل هذا بقوله لباعة الحمام «إرفعوا هذه من ههنا لا تجعلوا بيت أبي بيت تجارة فتذكر تلاميذه انه مكتوب غيرة

eaten Me up'" (Jn 2:16–17). He again established this when He entered Jerusalem publicly in a great celebration [Hosanna Sunday] (Mt 21:1–17). Since He was outright rejected and shunned by the Jews and their leaders, He left them and the place. This was to showcase that, "this house, the temple, which was built to honor the Lord and His name is only a place of worship in image and authority, and is not My house. I leave it to you desolate"; this accords with what God had told Solomon:

> But if you or your sons at all turn from following Me, and do not keep My commandments and My statutes which I have set before you, but go and serve other gods and worship them, then I will cut off Israel from the land which I have given them; and this house which I have consecrated for My name I will cast out of My sight. Israel will be a proverb and a byword among all peoples. And as for this house, which is exalted, everyone who passes by it will be astonished and will hiss, and say, "Why has the Lord done thus to this land and to this house?" Then they will answer, "Because they forsook the Lord their God, who brought their fathers out of the land of Egypt, and have embraced other gods, and worshiped them and served them; therefore the Lord has brought all this calamity on them." (1 Kg 9:6–9)

Judas' Treachery

On this Wednesday, Judas Iscariot, one of the disciples, went to the chief priests and asked them, "What are you willing to give me if I deliver Him to you?" (Mt 26:15). So they promised to give him 30 pieces of silver [the price of a slave], equivalent to 33 pennies. Judas sold his Master for this disgraceful value; He, who loved him, chose him as His disciple, and made him His treasurer. This happened to fulfill that which was spoken by the prophet: "'If it is agreeable to you, give me my wages; and if not, refrain.' So they weighed out for my wages thirty pieces of silver. And the Lord said to me, 'Throw it to the potter'—that princely price they set on me. So I took the thirty pieces of silver and threw them into the house of the Lord for the

بيتك أكلتنى» (يو٢: ١٦-١٧)، و قد أثبت ذلك أيضاً عند دخوله أورشليم علانية بالإحتفال العظيم (مت٢١: ١-١٧)، ولكن حيث أنه قد رُفِضَ من اليهود رفضاً باتاً وقاطعه الرؤساء فتركهم السيد المسيح له المجد وترك المكان الذى كان قد اختاره الرب ليضع إسمِه عليه الى الابد، وكأنه يقول إن البيت هذا الذى كان لى وأنتم جعلتم العبادة فيه صورية ريائية ليس هو بيتى الآن، فسأتركه لكم خراباً، وذلك وفقاً لما قاله الله له المجد قديماً لسليمان

«إن كنتم تنقلبون انتم او ابناؤكم من ورائي ولا تحفظون وصاياى فرائضى التى جعلتها أمامكم بل تذهبون وتعبدون آلهة أخرى وتسجدون لها، فاني أقطع اسرائيل عن وجه الارض التى اعطيتهم إياها والبيت الذى قدسته لاسمى انفيه من أمامى. ويكون اسرائيل مثلا وهزأة في جميع الشعوب، وهذا البيت يكون عبرة، كل من يمر عليه يتعجب ويصفر ويقولون لماذا عمل الرب هكذا لهذه الارض ولهذا البيت. فيقولون من أجل أنهم تركوا الرب الهم الذى أخرج أباءهم من أرض مصر وتمسكوا بآلهة أخرى وسجدوا لها وعبدوها لذلك جلب الرب عليهم كل هذا الشر» (١مل٩: ٦-٩).

خيانة يهوذا:

ففى هذا اليوم (الاربعاء) ذهب يهوذا الاسخريوطى أحد التلاميذ إلى رؤساء الكهنة وقال لهم ماذا تعطونى وأنا أُسلمه لكم؟ (مت ٢٦: ١٥)، فوعدوه أن يعطوه ثلاثين من الفضة تعادل ثلاثمائة وثلاثين قرشاً فباع سيده الذى أحبه وإنتخبه أن يكون له تلميذاً وصيره أميناً للصندوق بهذه القيمة الدنية. وكان هذا لكي يتم ما قيل بالنبي القائل «ان حسن في أعينكم فاعطوني أجرتي والا فامتنعوا، فوزنوا أجرتى ثلاثين من الفضة. فقال لي الرب إلقها الى الفخارى الثمن الكريم الذى ثمنونى به. فأخذت الثلاثين من الفضة والقيتها الى الفخارى فى بيت الرب» (زك١١: ١٢-١٣).

potter" (Zech 11:12–13).

Judas' Suicide

After Judas had betrayed Jesus to them, seeing that He was condemned, Judas tried to return the silver, the price he had received for his precious Master, saying:

> "I have sinned by betraying innocent blood." And they said, "What is that to us? You see to it!" Then he threw down the pieces of silver in the temple and departed, and went and hanged himself. But the chief priests took the silver pieces and said, "It is not lawful to put them into the treasury, because they are the price of blood." And they consulted together and bought with them the potter's field, to bury strangers in. Therefore that field has been called the Field of Blood to this day. (Mt 27:4–8)

What was spoken by David the Prophet was fulfilled in Judas:

> For the mouth of the wicked and the mouth of the deceitful have opened against me; they have spoken against me with a lying tongue. They have also surrounded me with words of hatred, and fought against me without a cause. In return for my love they are my accusers... Set a wicked man over him, and let an accuser stand at his right hand. When he is judged, let him be found guilty, and let his prayer become sin. Let his days be few, and let another take his office. Let his children be fatherless, and his wife a widow. Let his children continually be vagabonds, and beg; let them seek their bread also from their desolate places... Let his posterity be cut off, and in the generation following let their name be blotted out. Let the iniquity of his fathers be remembered before the Lord, and let not the sin of his mother be blotted out... As he loved cursing, so let it come to him; as he did not delight in blessing, so let it be far from him. As he clothed himself with cursing as with his garment, so let it enter his body like water, and like oil into his bones... Let this be the Lord's reward to my

إنتحاره:

وبعد ما اسلمه لهم رأى نفسه أنه قد دين فمضي لوقته ورد لهم الفضة التى أخذها منهم ثمن سيده الكريم قائلا

«قد أخطأت اذ سلمت دماً بريئاً». فقالوا ماذا علينا أنت أبصر. فطرح الفضة في الهيكل وانصرف. ثم مضي وخنق نفسه. فأخذ روساء الكهنة الفضة وقالوا لايحل ان نلقيها فى الخزانة لانها ثمن دم. فتشاوروا واشتروا بها حقل الفخاري مقبرة للغرباء. لهذا سمى هذا الحقل حقل دم الى هذا اليوم (مت ٢٧: ٤-٨).

فتم على يهوذا ما قيل على لسان داود النبى

«لانه قد انفتح على فم الشرير وفم الغش. تكلموا معى بلسان كذب. بكلام بغض احاطوا بى وقاتلونى بلا سبب، بدل محبتى يخاصموننى، فاقم انت عليه سريراً وليقف شيطاناً عن يمينه. اذا حوكم فليخرج مذنباً و صلاته فتكن خطية. تكن أيامه قليلة وأسقفيته يأخذها آخر. ليكن بنوه أيتاماً وامرأته أرملة. ليتيه بنوه تيهانا ويستعطوا. ويلتمسوا خبزاً من خربهم . . . لتنقرض ذريته فى الجيل القادم. ليُمح اسمهم ليُذكر اسم ابائه لدى الرب ولا تمح خطية أمه . . . فأحب اللعنة فاتته ولم يسر البركة فتباعدت عنه، ولبس اللعنة مثل الثوب ودخلت مثل الماء فى إمعائه وكزيت فى عظامه . . . هذه أجرة مبغضي من عند الرب وأجرة المتكلمين شراً على نفسى» (مز١٠٩ : ٢-٢٠)،

accusers, and to those who speak evil against my person (Ps 109:2–20).

The Book of Acts also mentions:

Men and brethren, this Scripture had to be fulfilled, which the Holy Spirit spoke before by the mouth of David concerning Judas, who became a guide to those who arrested Jesus; for he was numbered with us and obtained a part in this ministry. (Now this man purchased a field with the wages of iniquity; and falling headlong, he burst open in the middle and all his entrails gushed out. And it became known to all those dwelling in Jerusalem; so that field is called in their own language, Akel Dama, that is, Field of Blood.) For it is written in the book of Psalms: "Let his dwelling place be desolate, and let no one live in it"; and, "Let another take his office" (Acts 1:16–20).

Judas Deserves Punishment

One may ponder that, if it was necessary for the Lord Christ to be delivered to the Jews to be crucified (if not through Judas, it would have been through someone else), and if the Holy Scripture describe in great detail Judas' actions, then what was his fault, how did he sin, and why did he perish? The response is that our omniscient omnipresent God preceded and revealed to His servants the prophets the life events of the Savior on earth—beginning from the Annunciation of the Angel to the Virgin until His Ascension to heaven and the descent of the Holy Spirit upon the disciples. All who treated the Lord Christ, whether with good or evil deeds, did so freely, not by force or compulsion. God's foreknowledge was not the cause of people's actions. All the prophecies concerning Judas, Judas fulfilled freely, and willfully accomplished—he was the author of his life choices, which he made without coercion. He had no intention of fulfilling the prophecies. Even if this had been his intention, he still would have perished, because people have a choice to do that which is good and to avoid evil. God does not wish to take vengeance on a killer because he committed murder, as

وذُكِر أيضاً فى أعمال الرسل

«ايها الرجال الاخوة كان ينبغى ان يتم هذا المكتوب الذى سبق الروح القدس فقاله بفم داود عن يهوذا الذى صار دليلا للذين قبضوا على يسوع. اذ كان معدوداً بيننا وصارله نصيب فى هذه الخدمة. فأن هذا اقتنى حقلا من أجرة الظلم واذ سقط على وجهه انشق من الوسط فانسكبت أحشاؤه كلها. وصار ذلك معلوماً عند جميع سكان أورشليم حتى دُعى ذلك الحقل في لغتهم حقل دماً أى حقل دم. لانه مكتوب فى سفر المزامير لتصر داره خراباً ولا يكن فيها ساكن وليأخذ خدمته آخر» (أع١: ١٦-٢٠)

إستحقاقه العقاب:

يتبادر للذهن انه إذا كان لابد أن يسلم السيد المسيح لليهود ليصلب، وإن لم يكن بيهوذا كان سيكون بغيره، والنصوص الالهية تشير الى كل ما يعمله يهوذا فما هو ذنبه وما هى خطيته ولماذا يهلك، الجواب : ان الله له المجد العالم بكل شئ قبل كونه سبق فأوحى عن أفواه عبيده الانبياء كل حياة الفادى على الارض، وذلك من بدء بشارة الملاك للسيدة العذراء الى اليوم الذى إرتفع فيه الي السماء، وأرسل الروح القدس على التلاميذ. فكل الذين عاملوا السيد المسيح بالخير أو بالشر، عملوا ذلك مخيرين لا مسيرين. ولم يُرغموا على فعل ما أتوه. فعلم الله له المجد لم يكن سبباً في تصرفات هؤلاء الناس، لذلك الإنباء بيهوذا وبجميع ما يتعلق به فى كتب الانبياء كان قد فعله مخيراً ومريداً ولم يُرغم علي شئ منه، ولا فعل ذلك إتماماً لنبوات الانبياء. حتى لو كان قد فعل ذلك لكان أيضاً قد هلك، لأنه ينبغى للإنسان أن يفعل الصلاح ويتجنب الشر، لأن الله لا يريد أن ينتقم من القاتل كون أنه قاتل بل قال لقايين «الذي يقتلك ينتقم منه سبعة أضعاف» (تك٤: ١٥). فكم يكون من سلم دماً بريئاً

he said to Cain, "Whoever kills Cain, vengeance shall be taken on him sevenfold" (Gen 4:15). If so, then how much more shall the one who delivers honorable innocent blood, a Lamb without blemish, due to greed for thirty pieces of silver—a worldly profit? His punishment comes from Divine Justice for delivering his righteous Master.

Likewise, many, like Judas, sell their Master for even less than thirty pieces of silver. They pursue high profits by any means, defrauding by various ways until they fulfill their self-interest. They cheat, they lie, they flatter, they live without conscience, they become imposters, and they deceive innocent souls. They break the day of the Lord for the sake of a little money, the "root of all kinds of evil, for which some have strayed from the faith in their greediness, and pierced themselves through with many sorrows" (1 Tim 6:10). May God guard and protect us from this evil and keep us faithful until death. Amen.

Just Judgment of the Crucifiers

Some might question, if it were necessary for these events to happen to the Lord Christ when He came into the world, and if it had to be done through these specific people, then why does God judge them? The response is that their actions were provoked by the devil (the enemy of humanity), and were done through personal desire—meanwhile, their consciences bore witness to the Lord Christ. God will judge them for submitting to their desires; the judgment is just, whether passed on them or on others. It was not the Lord who asked them to crucify Him, or to fulfill the inevitable, but rather it was done of their own free will.

ومكرماً كما من حمل بلا عيب حباً في ثلاثين من الفضة إبتغاه للربح الدنيوى، فالعقاب الذى حل بيهوذا يستحقه، فهو صادر عن العدل الالهي لتسليمه لسيده البار.

وهكذا كثيرون كيهوذا يبيعون سيدهم المسيح بأقل مما باعه به يهوذا، فانهم يسعون وراء الكسب العالمى بأى طريق كان، ويتحايلون بشتى الطرق حتى يصلوا إلى أغراضهم، فتراهم يغشون ويكذبون ويتملقون ويعيشون بلا ضمير خداعين مغرورين بالنفوس البريئة، ويكسرون يوم الرب إبتغاءً لربح قليل من المال الذى هو أصل لكل الشرور، الذى إذا إبتغاه قوم ضلوا عن الإيمان وطعنوا أنفسهم بأوجاع كثيرة) ١ تى٦: ١٠(، وقانا الله وحمانا من ذلك وجعلنا أمناء إلى الموت آمين.

دينونة الصالبين العادلة:

وإن قال البعض إنه كان حتماً أن يتم بالسيد المسيح عند مجيئه الى العالم ما يتم، وإنه لابد أن يكون بغيرهم، فلماذا يدين الله هؤلاء؟ لأن ما فعله هؤلاء كان بإيعاز من إبليس عدو الإنسانية، وقد فعلوا ذلك إبتغاء لنوال شهوات بينما كانت ضمائرهم تشهد للسيد المسيح، فسيدينهم الله على إستسلامهم لشهوات نفوسهم، لأنهم عملوا أفعالهم إستسلاماً لشهواتهم وليس إتماماً للنبوات، فدينونتهم عادلة سواء كان هؤلاء أم غيرهم فإن الرب لم يطلب منهم أن يصلبوه أو أن يتمموا ما لابد أن يتم به.

HOLY COVENANT THURSDAY

بيان عن يوم الخميس الكبير من البصخة المقدسة

When it was the first day of Unleavened Bread, "when the Passover must be killed" (Lk 22:7), Jesus commanded two of his disciples to prepare the Passover for them to eat together. This is stated in the Gospel according to Saints Matthew, Mark, and Luke (Mt 26:17; Mk 14:12; Lk 22:8). In the afternoon, they went to the place where the disciples had prepared the Passover—the house of our teacher, St. Mark the Evangelist, as both tradition and the disciple himself reveal (Mk 14:13). On this said day, the fourteenth of the month of Nisan, the Jews refrained from work in the afternoon and removed all leaven from their homes (Ex 12:15). Preparations for the Passover are made on the fourteenth day, and hence, this day is called the first day of Unleavened Bread. At twilight (Lev 23:5), between afternoon and sunset, as the eve of the fifteenth day drew near, is when the slaughter of the Passover lamb takes place. On Thursday afternoon, our Savior returned once more to

ولما جاء اليوم الاول من الفطير الذي كان ينبغي أن يُذبح فيه الفصح (لو ٢٢: ٧)، أمر يسوع إثنين من تلاميذه أن يذهبا ويُعِدا الفصح ليأكله معهم جميعاً، كما هو واضح فى البشائر متى ومرقس ولوقا (مت٢٦: ١٧) ، (مر١٤ :١٢)، (لو٢٢: ٨)، وبعد الظهر توجه الي المكان الذى أعد التلاميذ فيه الفصح، فى بيت معلمنا مرقس الإنجيلي كما يُخبر التقليد، وكما يظهر لنا من نفس إنجيله (مر١٤: ١٣)، ثم أن اليوم المشار اليه هنا هو اليوم الرابع عشر من نيسان، الذى كان اليهود يكفون فيه عن الشغل عند الظهر، ويخرجون كل مختمر من البيوت (خر ١٢: ١٥) ثم بين العشائين (لا ٢٣: ٥)، أى بين العصر والغروب يذبحون فيه خروف الفصح، ومتى إبتدأ مساء اليوم الخامس عشر كانت الإستعدادات لذلك تُصنع فى اليوم الرابع عشر، ولهذا السبب كان يُدعى هذا اليوم « اليوم الاول من الفطير» وبعد ظهر يوم الخميس رجع مخلصنا له المجد مرة أخرى إلى أورشليم لا إلى الهيكل، ومعه تلاميذه

Jerusalem (but not to the temple) with His disciples to eat the Passover—the Jewish great feast commanded in chapter twelve of the Book of Exodus (Ex 12:1-14).

Passover Ritual

Pesah is a Hebrew word meaning "to pass over," which is in reference to the time when the angel of death passed over the children of Israel and killed the firstborn of the Egyptians. The duration of the feast was seven days (Ex 12:15), beginning on the fifteenth day of the month of Nisan and ending on the twenty-first day of Nisan (Ex 12:18; Lev 23:6; Num 28:17). By law, it was necessary for Jews, during this period, to eat only unleavened bread (Ex 12:15,18), and hence, the name The Feast of Unleavened Bread. There were five conditions for the feast:

1) Slaughter of the lamb.

2) Sprinkling the blood on the doorposts and lintel of the homes celebrating.

3) Roasting the whole lamb without breaking any bones (Ex 12:46), (symbolic of the Passion of the Lord Christ for our sake) (Jn 19:36).

4) Eating the lamb with unleavened bread and bitter herbs.

5) Not keeping any of it till morning (Ex 12:4–14).

Passover Eating Place

According to Jewish custom, groups of no less than ten persons and no more than twenty are formed when eating the Passover lamb. If the residents of one house were less than ten, the members of two houses shared one lamb. According to the law, each group delegated one person to bring the lamb to the temple and help the Levites to slaughter it, then, to bring it back to

ليأكل الفصح، وهو العيد العظيم عند اليهود الذى أُمِروا بعمله فى الإصحاح الثانى عشر من سفر الخروج (خر١٢: ١-١٤).

طقوس الفصح:

«الفصح» لفظة عبرانية معناها «العبور» يعنى بها عبور الملاك المُهلِك عن بنى إسرائيل حين قتل أبكار المصريين. وكانت مدة العيد سبعة أيام (خر١٢: ١٥) تبتدئ من اليوم الخامس عشر من شهر نيسان وتنتهي في الحادى والعشرين منه (خر١٢: ١٨)، (لا ٢٣: ٦)، (عدد ٢٨: ١٧)، وكان محتماً على اليهود بمقتضى الناموس الا يأكلوا فى هذه المدة سوى الفطير (خر١٢: ١٥، ١٨)، ولذلك سمى بعيد الفطير. وتستلزم ممارسة الفصح خمسة أمور:

١. ذبح الخروف

٢. رش الدم على قائمتى الباب وعتبته من بيت المعبد.

٣. شي الخروف صحيحاً من دون أن يُكسر منه عظم (خر١٢: ٤٦)، وفى ذلك رمز إلى الآم السيد المسيح من أجلنا (يو١٩: ٣٦).

٤. أكله مع الفطير والآعشاب المرة.

٥. عدم إبقاء شىء منه الي الصبح (خر١٢: ٤-١٤).

مكان أكله:

كان من عوائد اليهود أن يقسموا أنفسهم في أكل خروف الفصح إلى جماعات كل منها لا تقل عن عشرة أشخاص ولا تتجاوز العشرين شخصاً. فإن لم يبلغ سكان البيت الواحد العشرة أشخاص إشترك بيتان فى خروف واحد، وكان كل جماعة تنيب عنها واحداً ليُحضر الخروف إلى دار الهيكل، ويساعد أيضاً اللاويين على ذبحه، ثم ينقل

the house where they intended to eat it (Lev 12:4-14). For this Passover, the disciples, Peter and John, achieved this on behalf of our Savior and His disciples (Lk 22:8). They prepared the bread, wine, bitter herbs, and all the necessities for the Passover. The disciples inquired of the Lord where they could eat the Passover. Therefore, when they had asked Jesus, He sent two of them with a sign to identify the owner of the house—a man "carrying a pitcher of water" (Mk 14:13). Our Savior wisely hid the location from His disciples until the hour came in which it was time to feast. He did this to prevent Judas from informing the Jewish leaders, who intended to arrest and detain Him, until after the feast. He only informed Peter and John. And only after they had completed all necessary preparations, Jesus arrived with the rest of the disciples (who did not know the whereabouts of the feast) and ate the Passover.

The Four Passover Cups

In the Jewish custom, four cups of red wine mixed with a little water were consumed at dinner. The host would bless saying, "Blessed be Thou, O Lord our God, eternal King, who creates the fruit of the vine," and drank the inaugural glass.[35] This was called the cup of bitterness, as mentioned in the Gospel according to St. Luke (Lk 22:17). Afterward, they would wash, symbolic of their ancestors' crossing of the Red Sea, and then, they would approach to eat what was set before them on the table—the bitter herbs, unleavened bread, roasted lamb, date soup, almonds, figs, raisins, vinegar, cinnamon, and other spices. Next, the host would take some of the herbs to dip in the soup and eat. As he does this, he thanks God, who created the bounties of the earth, and the guests in return would answer him saying, "Amen." Following this, a boy would come forward and ask his father about the reason for keeping these laws, and his father in turn would respond by saying that the slaughter of the sheep was a reminder of the angel of death, who passing over the houses of the Hebrews did not harm them. The unleavened bread symbolizes the bread of affliction, which they ate unleavened as they fled from Pharaoh (Deut 16:3), the bitter herbs

ما يُذبح إلى البيت الذى يقصدون أن يأكلوه فيه حسب الشريعة (خر١٢: ٤-١٤)، وقد قام بذلك في الهيكل هذه المرة بالنيابة عن مخلصنا تلاميذه بطرس ويوحنا (لو٢٢: ٨)، وأعدا الخبز والخمر والاعشاب المرة وكل ما هو ضرورياً لإعداد الفصح. ولم يفهم التلاميذ المكان الذى سيأكلون فيه الفصح، ولذا سألوه عنه، فأرسل إثنين منهم وأعطاهما علامة يميزان بها صاحب ذلك البيت. وهو انسان حامل جرة ماء (مر ١٤: ١٣)، وكان لمخلصنا حكمة في إخفاء معرفة المكان عن تلاميذه إلى تلك الساعة حتى لا يتمكن يهوذا من أن يُعلم جماعة اليهود به فيقبضوا عليه ويحفظوه عندهم إلى ما بعد العيد. فأطلع بطرس ويوحنا فقط على ذلك. ولما أعدا كل شئ وجاءا به، ذهب هو وتلاميذه الذين لم يكونوا يعرفون المكان حتى دخلوه فاكلوا الفصح هناك.

كؤوسه الأربع:

كان لليهود عادة أن يشربوا على العشاء أربعة كؤوس خمرٍ حمراء ممزوجة بقليل من الماء:

الكأس الأول تُدعى «كأس المرارة» ويُعتبر إفتتاحية، فيأخذه رئيس الجماعة ويباركه قائلاً: «فليكن الرب مباركاً الذى أبدع ثمر الكرمة»[٣٥]. ، وهو الكأس المذكورة فى إنجيل لوقا (لو٢٢: ١٧) وعلى أثر ذلك كانوا يغتسلون وهذا الإغتسال كانوا يشيرون بها الى عبور أسلافهم البحر الاحمر. ثم يتقدمون الى المائدة لأكل ما قد أعد عليها من الأعشاب المرة و الفطير والخروف المشوى والمرق المصنوع من البلح، واللوز والتين والزبيب والخل والقرفة وغيرها من البهارات و أيضاً خجيجة اليوم الرابع عشر. وحينئذ يأخذ رئيس الجماعة شيئاً من الأعشاب ويغمسه فى المرق، ويأكله شاكراً الله الذى أبدع خيرات الأرض، فيجاوبه باقى المتكئين قائلين آمين. وعقب ذلك يتقدم ولد ويسأل والده عن سبب حفظ هذه الفريضة، فيجيبه على ذلك أن ذبح الخروف هو تذكار لمرور الملاك المبيد أمام بيوت العبرانيين بدون أن يؤذِهم. والفطير يشير الى خبز الشدة الذى أكلوه فطيراً وقت هروبهم من أمام فرعون (تث ١٦: ٣)، والأعشاب المرة

symbolize the slavery, which they suffered in Egypt, and the soup (with its color and thickness) symbolizes the cities of Pithom and Raamses, which their ancestors built for Pharaoh as forced laborers (Ex 1:11; Deut 6:20).

Thereafter, they would say the first part of the praise, Psalms 113 and 114, and drink the second cup, which they call the cup of joy, begging for a blessing upon each type of food. The host would then take the unleavened bread, break it, and distribute it to the guests, who would dip it into the soup until they have fully consumed it. Sometimes, the host would dip the piece of bread in the dish (as our Savior did) and give to each one of the guests. Once this is done, they conclude their meal by eating the Passover lamb, of which they leave no remainders.

Then, they offer thanksgiving and drink the third cup, which is called the cup of blessing (1 Cor 10:16), and they sing the remainder of the hymn of praise, which is "Not unto us, O Lord, not unto us, but to Your name give glory" (Ps 115:1).

Drinking the fourth cup usually concludes the celebration. Sometimes, they drank a fifth cup after singing the great hymn that contains seventeen psalms, from Psalm 120 to Psalm 136.

Washing of the Feet

At this time, a dispute occurred between the disciples as to which of them is the first and greatest, and each one tried to elevate himself, but Jesus addressed these vain thoughts: "And He said to them, 'The kings of the Gentiles exercise lordship over them, and those who exercise authority over them are called "benefactors." But not so among you; on the contrary, he who is greatest among you, let him be as the younger, and he who governs as he who serves'" (Lk 22:24–26). Instantly He arose and washed each disciple's feet. Peter was overwhelmed by the grandeur of this situation, and felt that he did not deserve this amazing act, so he told his Master, "'You shall never wash my feet!' Jesus answered him, 'If I do not wash you, you

رمـز إلي العبوديـة التـى كابدوهـا بمـصر، والمـرق المختـثر يمثـل بلونـه وخثورتـه طـين مدينتـى فيثـوم ورعمسـيس اللتـين بناهـا أسـلافهم لفرعـون بالتسـخير (خـر١: ١١)، (تـث٦: ٢٠).

ثـم يقولـون الجـزء الاول مـن التسـبيح وهـو المزمـور رقـم ١١٣ و رقـم ١١٤. بعـد ذلـك يشربـون الـكأس الثانيـة التـى يدعونهـا «كأس الفـرح» و يطلبـون البركـة عـلى كل نـوع مـن الطعـام، فيأخـذ الرئيـس الفطـير ويكسره و يوزعـه عـلى المتكئـين، فيأكلونـه بعـد أن يغمسـوه هـو و بالمـرق حتـى ينتهـي. وأحيانـاً يَغمـس الرئيـس الكـسر فى الصحفـة كـما فعـل مخلصلنـا لـه المجـد وناولهـم. ومتـى فرغـوا مـن ذلـك يأكلـون خـروف الفصـح ولا يبقـوا منـه شـيئاً ولا يأكلـون بعـده طعامـاً آخـر.

بعـد ذلـك يقدمـون تشـكرات وهـم يشربـون الـكأس الثالثـة التـى تدعـى «كأس البركـة» (١كـو ١٠: ١٦)، ثـم يرتلـون مـا بقـى مـن ترنيمـة التسـبيح وهـي "ليـس لنـا يـارب ليـس لنـا لكـن لاسـمك أعطـى مجـداً (مـز١١٥: ١).

ثـم يشربـون الـكأس الرابعـة التـى كانـوا غالبـاً يختمـون بهـا الاحتفـال. وأحيانـاً كانـوا يشربـون كأسـاً خامسـة بعـد ترنيمـة التسبحة العظيمـة المحتويـة عـلي سـبعة عـشر مزمـوراً وهـى مـن مزمـور ١٢٠ إلى مزمـور ١٣٦.

غسل الأرجل:

حدثـت فى هـذا الوقـت مشـاجرة بـين التلاميـذ فيمـن يظـن أن يكـون الاول والاعظـم، وحـاول كل واحـد منهـم أن يجعـل نفسـه الاول، فأنبهـم يسـوع عـلي تلـك الافـكار الباطلـة «فقـال لهـم ملـوك الامـم يسـودونهم والمتسـلطون عليهـم يدعـون محسـنين وأمـا أنتـم فليـس هكـذا بـل الكبـير فيكـم ليكـن كالصغـير والمتقـدم كالخـادم» (لـو٢٢: ٢٤-٢٦) وفى الحـال قـد قـام بعمليـة غسـل أرجـل التلاميـذ واحـداً واحـداً. أمـا بطـرس فاسـتعظم هـذ الامـر الكبـير ورأى نفسـه انـه لا يسـتحق هـذا الفعـل المدهـش، فقـال لسـيده لـن تغسـل رجـليّ أبـداً، فأجابـه يسـوع أن كنـت لا أغسـلك فليـس لـك معـى نصيـب. فخـاف بطـرس

have no part with Me.' Simon Peter said to Him, 'Lord, not my feet only, but also my hands and my head!'" (Jn 13:8–9).

Judas' Betrayal

After this, He alerted them to His betrayal by saying, "One of you will betray me" (Jn 13:21), meaning Judas, into whom Satan entered after he had received the morsel. Then, Jesus addressed Judas directly: "What you do, do quickly" (Jn 13:27). Judas arose immediately and went to the Jews to deliver to them his Master. He guided them and was an accomplice to them in the Lord Jesus' arrest, in return for thirty shekels of silver. Each shekel equals thirteen and a half Egyptian pounds; therefore, thirty shekels equal four hundred and five cents—the price of a slave (Ex 21:32) at that time. The Lord Christ was sold to die as a slave in order to free us from the yoke of bitter bondage. Zechariah prophesied concerning this, saying, "'If it is agreeable to you, give me my wages; and if not, refrain.' So they weighed out for my wages thirty pieces of silver" (Zech 11:12).

What a vast difference between Mary's valuation of the Lord Christ and Judas' valuation of Him! At the dinner, she washed His feet with perfume that was valued at three hundred dinars to honor Him (Jn 12:5). On the contrary, Judas betrayed Jesus for a mere four hundred and five cents.

Lessons from His Betrayal

From Judas' story, we can learn several lessons:

1) Gaining the greatest means does not guarantee salvation. Judas was a chosen disciple, one of the twelve, accompanying Christ, witnessing His miracles, hearing His teachings, a partner to Peter, James, and John, and having received from the means of grace what Abraham, Moses, Isaiah, and Daniel did not receive. He perished because he did not remove greed from his heart.

وقال ياسيد ليس رجلىّ فقط بل يدى ورأسى (يو١٣: ٨- ٩).

خيانة يهوذا:

بعد ذلك أنبأهم بخيانة يهوذا بقوله -له المجد- إن واحداً منكم يسلمنى (يو١٣: ٢١)، يقصد به يهوذا الذى إذ بعد أن أخذ اللقمة دخله الشيطان. فقال له يسوع ما أنت تعمله فأعمله بأكثر سرعة (يو١٣ : ٢٧)، فقام فى الحال ومضى إلى اليهود ليسلم لهم سيده بالارشاد عليه والاشتراك معهم فى القبض عليه أيضاً مقابل إعطائه ثلاثين من الفضة أى ثلاين شاقلاً من الفضة، والشاقل يساوى ثلاثة عشر قرشاً ونصف قرش من النقود المصرية، فيكون المبلغ الذى أخذه أربعمائة وخمس قروش، وهذه القيمة كانت ثمن العبد (خر٢١: ٣٢) فى ذلك الوقت، فبيع السيد المسيح للموت كعبد لكى يحررنا من نير العبودية الدائمة للخطية والموت. وتنبأ زكريا عن ذلك بقوله «إن حسن في أعينكم فاعطوني أجرتي وإلا فامتنعوا، فوزنوا أجرتي ثلاثين من الفضة»(زك١١: ١٢).

فما أعظم الفرق بين قيمة السيد المسيح عند مريم وقيمته عند يهوذا، فإنها أنفقت على إكرامه عند العشاء ثلثمائة دينار (يو١٢: ٥)، وباعه يهوذا للموت بأقل من ثلث هذه القيمة أى باربعمائة وخمس قروش.

دروس من خيانته:

فنتعلم من قصة يهوذا جملة الفوائد الآتية:

أولاً: إن الحصول على أفضل الوسائط لا يتكفل وحده بالخلاص، فإن يهوذا كان رسولا مختاراً من ضمن الاثنى عشر و كان رفيقاً للمسيح، وشاهد معجزاته وسمع تعاليمه، وكان شريكاً لبطرس ويعقوب ويوحنا، ونال من وسائط النعمة مالم ينله ابراهيم وموسي وأشعياء ودانيال، ومع كل ذلك فانه هلك، لانه لم ينزع

2) A person might gain a good reputation among people, but have no godliness before God. The Lord Christ sent Judas, just as He commissioned the rest of the disciples, to teach and perform miracles, so he appeared to have left everything for the sake of Christ, like his companions. None suspected him because he was appointed treasurer to the moneybox. When the Master told the apostles, "One of you will betray Me" (Mt 26:21; Jn 13:21), none thought of Judas, but each one suspected himself, as each one asked, "Lord, is it I?" (Mt 26:22).

3) The love of money is a great danger and a dark wickedness; Judas was conspicuous in his love of money. This is evident in his words to the chief priests, "What are you willing to give me if I deliver Him to you?" (Mt 26:15). Yes, Judas left much when he followed Jesus, yet he did not leave behind his greed, so he perished and drowned in despair, as a ship drowns for having a small hole within it. We see that Judas is not the only example. The love of money caused Delilah to deliver her husband Samson to the Philistines. It caused Gehazi to deceive Naaman and lie to Elisha, and so he was struck with leprosy. It caused Ananias and Sapphira to lie to the Holy Spirit, and so, they perished. It caused Judas to carry out the most heinous sin—betraying the Son of God to His murderers, so he hanged himself: "For the love of money is a root of all kinds of evil, for which some have strayed from the faith in their greediness, and pierced themselves through with many sorrows" (1 Tim 6:10). This fulfills the Lord Christ's words: "From him who does not have, even what he has will be taken away" (Mt 25:29).

4) Being disappointed by friends is no wonder, as the Lord Christ personally tasted the bitterness of this cup–the cup of betrayal by friends, and so, is able to sympathize with us (Heb 4:15). In fact, it is rare to find a friend upon whom one can rely in times of distress.

5) The most wicked enmity Christ suffered came from those closest to Him, as mentioned in the Book of Psalms (Ps 41:9; 55:12–14). This

الطمع من نفسه.

ثانياً: يمكن أن ينال الإنسان صيتاً حسناً بين الناس وهو بلا تقوى أمام الله، فالسيد المسيح أرسل يهوذا كسائر الرسل ليعلم ويصنع الآيات، فظهر أنه ترك كل شئ لأجل المسيح كغيره من الرسل، ولم يظن أحد منهم سوءاً لأنهم عينوه أميناً للصندوق، وحينما قال السيد للرسل «واحد منكم يسلمنى» (مت ٢٦: ٢١)، (يو١٣: ٢١) لم يفكر أحد فى يهوذا بل نظر كل واحد الى نفسه أولا، بدليل قول كل واحد منهم «هل أنا يارب» (مت ٢٦: ٢٢).

ثالثاً: إن محبة المال خطر عظيم وشر جسيم، ويهوذا كان من أول محبى المال، ويدل على ذلك قوله لرؤساء الكهنة «ماذا تريدون أن تعطونى وأنا أسلمه إليكم»(مت٢٦: ١٥). نعم إن يهوذا ترك كثيراً عندما تبع يسوع، ولكنه لم يترك طمعه فأهلكه وأغرقه فى لجة اليأس كما تغرق السفينة بواسطة ثقب صغير فيها. ولم يكن مثال يهوذا هو المثل الوحيد فحب المال حمل دليلة على تسليم زوجها شمشون الى الفلسطينيين، وحمل جيحزى على خداع نعمان والكذب على إليشع، وحمل حنانيا وسفيرة على أن يكذبا على الروح القدس، وهكذا حمل يهوذا على أن يرتكب أفظع الآثام وهو تسليم إبن الله الى قاتليه. فعلينا أن نصغى الى قول الرسول «محبة المال أصل لكل الشرور الذى إذا إبتغاه قوم ضلوا عن الإيمان وطعنوا أنفسهم بأوجاع كثيرة» (١تى٦: ١٠) وهذا يحقق قول السيد المسيح «ومن ليس له فالذى عنده يؤخذ منه»(مت ٢٥: ٢٩).

رابعاً: إنه لا عجب من خيبة الأمل فى الأصحاب. لان السيد المسيح نفسه ذاق مرارة هذه الكأس، كأس خيانة الاصدقاء، وصار بذلك قادراً على أن يشعر بنا ويرثي لنا فى تلك الأحوال (عب ٤: ١٥). وفى الحقيقة أنه قلَّ أن يوجد صديق حقيقى يركن اليه الانسان فى أوقات الضيق.

خامساً: إن شر أعداء المسيح كان من أقرب أصحابه كما جاء فى سفر المزامير

harmed the Church (the body of Christ) in every age, more so than external enemies. Likewise, a person is not usually harmed, except from those closest to him—his friends. This is seen and encountered on a daily basis, as the Holy Bible explicitly says, "A man's enemies are the men of his own household" (Mic 7:6; Mt 10:36).

6) Sometimes, good results from evil; Judas' outcome was the greatest evidence confounding the false accusations against Christ. After he betrayed Him, he could have silenced his conscience and the accusations of others by remembering some faults in Christ (who was flawless), yet, instead we find that he cast down in the treasury the silver which he had taken as payment for his monstrous act, saying, "I have sinned by betraying innocent blood" (Mt 27:4). This silences those who claim that we have no witness to Christ's innocence, except the testimony of His friends.

7) Relenting over evil, after the fact, is unbeneficial and does not restore the damage, unless it is by true repentance. Although Judas repented, returned the coins, and confessed his sins, yet, he was unable to save Christ, because they did not acknowledge him with an answer, except, "What is that to us? You see to it!" (Mt 27:4). Neither was he able to silence his conscience as revealed by the fact that he "went and hanged himself" (Mt 27:5). This is because he did not resort to his Master with true relenting and repentance accompanied by tears, as Peter did, who "went out and wept bitterly" (Mt 26:75; Lk 22:62), and so, the Lord forgave Peter's sins.

Instituting the Thanksgiving (Eucharist) Mystery

The Lord Christ instituted the Mystery of the Holy Eucharist [the Lord's Supper]: "The bread of God is He who comes down from heaven and gives life to the world" (Jn 6:33)—His holy Body and precious Blood—replacing the symbol with the essence it resembles. He entrusted to His disciples a

(مز٤١: ٩) ، (٥٥: ١٢-١٤) وهـذه أضرت بالكنيسـة التـى هـى «جسـد المسيح» فى كل عـصر أكـثر مـن كل الأعـداء الخارجـين عليهـا. وكذلـك ضرر الانسـان لا يلحقـه غالبـاً إلا مـن أقاربـه وأصحابـه كـما هـو مشـاهد ومحسـوس يوميـاً. وكـما يقـول الكتـاب بصريـح العبـارة أن أعـداء الانسـان أهـل بيتـه (مـي ٧: ٦)، (مـت ١٠: ٣٦) والمقربـون اليـه.

سادسـاً: أنـه فى بعـض الأحيـان قـد ينتـج مـن الـشر خـير، فـإن عاقبـة خيانـة يهـوذا كانـت أفضـل برهـان عـلى صحـة دعـوى المسـيح، لأنـه بعدمـا سـلمه كان عليـه أن يُسـكت ضمـيره ويُسـكت توبيـخ الآخريـن لـه بذكـر شئ مـن عيـوب المسـيح الـذى لم يكـن فيـه عيـب. ولكنـا رأينـاه يطـرح فى الخزانـة الفضـة التـى كان قـد أخذهـا أجـرة عـلى إثمـه قائـلاً «أخطـأت إذ سـلمت دمـاً بريئـاً» (مـت ٢٧: ٤) وهـذا يفحـم مـن يقـول ليـس لنـا شـهادة بـر المسـيح سـوى شـهادة أصحابـه.

سـابعاً: إن الندامـة عـلى الـشر بعـد إتيانـه لا تفيـد شـيئاً ولا تصلـح ماقـد فسـد إلا إذا كانـت مـن خـلال توبـة حقيقيـة، فـإن يهـوذا نـدم ورد الدراهـم وإعـترف بإثمـه ولكنـه لم يقـدر أن ينقـذ المسـيح، لأنهـم لم يجيبـوه إلا بقولهـم «مـاذا علينـا أنـت أبـصر» (مـت ٢٧: ٤)، ولم يسـتطع أن يسـكت ضمـيره بدليـل أنـه «مـضى وخنـق نفسـه» (مـت ٢٧: ٥) وذلـك لأنـه لم يلجـأ الى سـيده بالندامـة والتوبـة الحقيقيـة المشـفوعة بالدمـوع كـما فعـل بطـرس» فإنـه بـكى بـكاءً مـراً» (مـت ٢٦: ٧٥)، (لـو٢٢: ٦٢) فغفـر لـه الـرب خطايـاه.

رسم سر الشكر:

ثـم رسـم لهـم العشـاء الربـانى وهـو الخبـز النـازل مـن السـماء الواهـب حيـاة للعـالم (يـو٦: ٣٣). أى جسـده المقـدس ودمـه الكريـم، حيـث أبطـل أمامـم الرمـز، وأشـار لهـم

New Covenant, instead of the Old Covenant, as the Evangelists described in their accounts of the Holy Gospel: "And as they were eating (the Passover), Jesus took bread, blessed and broke it, and gave it to them and said… 'Take, eat; this is My body which is broken for you; do this in remembrance of Me.' … Likewise He also took the cup after supper, saying, 'This cup is the new covenant in My blood, which is shed for you'" (Mk 14:22–25, 1 Cor 11:24-25, Lk 22:20). This is besides the first cup mentioned by St. Luke: "Then He took the cup, and gave thanks, and said, 'Take this and divide it among yourselves; for I say to you, I will not drink of the fruit of the vine until the kingdom of God comes'" (Lk 22:17-18). The first meal and drink were the Passover supper, but the second bread and cup are the New Covenant that is given for the remission of sins.

After the Passover supper, the Lord's Supper [Holy Eucharist], and transmitting to the disciples this great Mystery, He foretold and emphasized Peter's trice denial of Him. Then, He arose with His disciples and crossed over and entered the Kidron Valley where He prayed strenuously to the point that His sweat fell to the ground like great drops of blood, and an angel appeared to Him from heaven strengthening Him (Lk 22:43–44), saying, "Thine is the power, the glory, the blessing, and the majesty, O Emmanuel our God and King." This is the only Church hymn chanted during Holy Week.

Evidence of the Changing of the Bread and Wine

The Lord's body and blood, which He handed to His disciples on that night, are His holy body and blood appearing as bread and wine. This is clearly evident to us from the following:

1) From the Lord Christ's own words, when He told the Jews, "'Moses gave your fathers bread in the wilderness, so they ate and are dead, yet My Father gives you the true Bread from heaven. The bread of God comes down from heaven and gives life of the world.' They said to Him, "Master, give us this bread continually.' Jesus said to them, 'I Am

إلى المرموز اليه. بل قد سلمه لهم عوضاً عنه عهداً جديداً غير العهد الاول. كما يوضح الانجيليون ذلك فى أناجيلهم قائلين، وفيما هم يأكلون -أى يأكلون الفصح- أخذ يسوع خبزاً وبارك وكسر وأعطاهم قائلاً: «خذوا كلوا هذا هو جسدي الذى يبذل عنكم إصنعوا هذا لذكرى. وكذلك الكأس أيضاً بعد العشاء قائلاً هذه الكأس هى العهد الجديد بدمى الذى يسفك عنكم، وهذه غير الكأس الأولى التى قال عنها لوقا (مر١٤: ٢٢-٢٥)، (لو٢٢: ٢٠)، (١كو١١: ٢٤-٢٥). ثم تناول كأساً وشكر وقال «خذوا هذه واقتسموها بينكم لانى أقول لكم إننى لا أشرب من نتاج الكرمة حتى يأتى ملكوت الله (لو٢٢: ١٧-١٨). فالأكل الاول والكأس الاولى هما «عشاء الفصح». أما الخبز الثانى والكأس الثانية فهما «العهد الجديد» الذي يُعطى لمغفرة الخطايا.

ثم بعد العشاء الفصحى وتناول العشاء الرباني و تسليم التلاميذ هذا السر العظيم، أنبأ له المجد بإنكار بطرس إياه الثلاث المرات، وأكد ذلك، ثم قام وذهب الى عبر وادى قدرون حيث دخل هو وتلاميذه، وهناك صلي بجهاد عظيم، حتى كان عرقه يتصبب كقطرات دم على الارض. وقد ظهر للسيد المسيح ملاك من السماء يقويه (لو٢٢: ٤٣-٤٤) قائلاً له «لك القوة، لك المجد، لك البركة، لك العزة يا عمانوئيل الهنا وملكنا». وهى ترنيمة الكنيسة الوحيدة أيام أسبوع الآلام.

أدلة إستحالة الخبز والخمر:

أما جسد الرب ودمه اللذان سلمهما لتلاميذه فى تلك الليلة، فهما جسده ودمه الأقدسين تحت أعراض الخبز والخمر، وهذا يتبرهن لنا جلياً فى الآتى:

أولاً: من أقوال الرب يسوع نفسه، حيث قال لليهود «إن موسى أعطى أبائكم الخبز فى البرية فأكلوه وماتوا، ولكن أبي يعطيكم الخبز الحقيقى من السماء، لأن خبز الله هو النازل من السماء الواهب الحياة الى للعالم، فقالوا له يا سيد أعطنا فى كل حين هذا الخبز، فقال لهم يسوع أنا هو خبز الحياة، من يقبل الىَّ

the bread of life. Whoever comes to Me will not hunger, and whoever believes in Me will never thirst. I Am the living bread coming down from heaven. If anyone eats of this bread, he will live forever. The bread that I give is My Body, which I shed for the life of the world. Whoever eats My flesh and drinks My blood has eternal life, and I will raise him up at the last day. For My flesh is food indeed, and My blood is drink indeed. He who eats My flesh and drinks My blood abides in Me, and I in him... he who feeds on Me will live because of Me'" (Cf. Jn 6:32-57).

2) His words to them as He handed them the New Covenant saying, "This is My body which is given for you... This cup is... My blood, which is shed for you" (Lk 22:19, 20).

3) The words of the Holy Spirit on the mouth of our teacher Paul the Apostle: "For he who eats and drinks in an unworthy manner eats and drinks judgment to himself, not discerning the Lord's body... [being] guilty of the body and blood of the Lord" (1 Cor 11:29, 27).

Leavened Bread

Just as the Lord Christ used, and as the Evangelists mention that He took leavened bread (Artos in Greek), the Body must also be of leavened bread made of pure wheat. The apostles also used leavened bread, as is witnessed in the Book of Acts (Act 2:42,46; 20:7,11, 27:35; 1 Cor 10:16–17, 11:23-27), where bread is mentioned, but not once is unleavened bread mentioned. The Holy Orthodox Church followed through in upholding this standard of using leavened bread in this Holy Mystery.

The blood also must be from pure grape juice, in order to resemble the shed Blood of the Lord Christ. This was prophesied by Jacob the Patriarch (being inspired by the Holy Spirit) concerning his son, Judah (from whose tribe the Lord descended): "He washed his garments in wine, and his clothes in the blood of grapes" (Gen 49:11).

فلا يجوع ومن يؤمن بى فلا يعطش إبداً، أنا هو الخبز الحى الذى نزل من السماء، إن أكل أحد من هذا الخبز يحيا الى الأبد، والخبز الذى أنا أعطى هو جسدى الذى أبذله من أجل حياة العالم، من يأكل جسدى ويشرب دمى فله حياة أبدية وأنا أقيمه فى اليوم الأخير، لأن جسدى مأكل حق ودمى مشرب حق، من يأكل جسدى ويشرب دمى يثبت فىَّ وأنا فيه، من يأكلنى يحيا بى» (يو ٦: ٣٢-٥٧).

ثانياً: من قوله لهم عند تسليمه إياهم للعهد الجديد حيث صرخ لهم قائلاً «هذا هو جسدى الذى يبذل عنكم وهذا هو دمى الذى يسفك من أجلكم (لو٢٢: ١٩-٢٠).

ثالثاً: ما قاله الروح القدس على لسان معلمنا بولس الرسول، من حيث من يأكل ويشرب بدون إستحقاق يأكل ويشرب دينونة لنفسه غير مميز جسد الرب، ثم قال أيضاً يكون مجرماً فى جسد الرب ودمه (١كو١١: ٢٧، ٢٩).

الخبز المختمر:

ويشترط أن يكون الجسد من خبز مختمر، مصنوع من القمح النقى. كما إستعمله الرب يسوع نفسه حيث يقول الانجيليون أخذ خبزاً، (أرطوس باليونانية أى خبز مختمر)، وقد إستعمله الرسل أيضاً بدليل ما جاء فى سفر الاعمال (أع٢: ٤٢، ٤٦)، (أع٢٠: ٧، ١١)، (أع٢٧: ٣٥)، (١كو١٠: ١٦-١٧)، (١كو١١: ٢٣-٢٧)، حيث يذكر خبزاً ولم يذكر ولا مرة واحدة كلمة فطير. وعلى هذا المثال صارت الكنيسة الارثوذكسية المقدسة تمارس هذا السر بالخبز المختمر.

أما الدم فيجب أن يكون من عصير العنب الخالص لكى يكون مماثلا لدم السيد المسيح المسفوك. كما تنبأ يعقوب أبو الآباء بالروح القدس عن يهوذا إبنه الذي طلع الرب من سبطه «غسل بالخمر لباسه وبدم العنب ثوبه»(تك ٤٩: ١١).

During the Divine Liturgy, the wine is mixed with water, as the Lord also mixed the wine during the Passover, as well as to commemorate the blood and water that flowed from the Redeemer's side on the cross (Jn 19:34). The Holy Spirit uttered of old, on the tongue of Solomon in his Proverbs concerning the Church: "She has slaughtered her meat, she has mixed her wine, she has also furnished her table" (Prov 9:2).

Labeling the Mystery a Sacrifice

This Mystery is called a "Holy Sacrifice," because it is the sacrificed body of the Lord Christ and His shed blood, since the Lord Christ became a sacrifice for us. He clearly stated that His body, which is sacrificed for the life of the world, is this bread (Jn 6:51), and His blood, which is shed for us, is this wine (Mt 26:28; Mk 14:24; Lk 22:20). As He became the Lamb of God who was sacrificed, and purchased us with His blood to God His Father, taught us to commemorate Him, teaching us this great Mystery. Therefore, when we observe it, we call it a Sacrifice. What is better than the words of St. Paul in his epistle to the Corinthians, when he said, "Observe Israel after the flesh: Are not those who eat of the sacrifices partakers of the altar? What am I saying then? That an idol is anything, or what is offered to idols is anything? Rather, that the things which the Gentiles sacrifice they sacrifice to demons and not to God, and I do not want you to have fellowship with demons. You cannot drink the cup of the Lord and the cup of demons; you cannot partake of the Lord's table and of the table of demons" (1 Cor 10:18-21). In these verses, the apostle compares the table of the Lord, the Christian altar, with the table of the Gentiles and the altar of demons. Thus, he confirms that what is offered on the Christian altar in the Divine Eucharistic Mystery is a true Sacrifice before God.

Benefits of Partaking of Communion

As for the benefits reaped by the believers who communicate this Mystery worthily, they are very many:

ثم يمزج الخمر عند الخدمة بالماء كما فعل السيد له المجد، وذلك كتذكار للدم والماء اللذين قد خرجا من جنب الفادى وهو علي الصليب (يو١٩: ٣٤) ، وقد نطق الروح القدس قديماً على لسان سليمان فى أمثاله عن الكنيسة قائلاً: «ذبحت ذبحها ومزجت خمرها، أيضاً رتبت مائدتها»(أم ٩: ٢).

تسمية السر ذبيحة:

يسمى هذا السر «ذبيحة مقدسة» لأنه جسد السيد المسيح المبذول ودمه المسفوك حيث أن السيد المسيح صار ذبيحة عنا. وقد وضح لنا بصريح العبارة أن جسده الذى سيبذله عن حياة العالم هو هذا الخبز (يو٦: ٥١)، وأن دمه الذى سيسفكه عنا هو هذا الخمر (مت ٢٦: ٢٨)، (مر ١٤: ٢٤)، (لو٢٢: ٢٠)، وكما صار هو حمل الله الذي ذبح وإشترانا بدمه لله أبيه ، وعلمنا أن نصنع ذكره يعلمنا هذا السر المقدس، فإذاً عندما نباشر تتميمه ندعوه ذبيحة، وما أحسن ما نطق به بولس الرسول فى رسالته لأهل كورنثوس حيث قال «إنظروا إسرائيل حسب الجسد أليس الذين يأكلون الذبائح هم شركاء المذبح فماذا أقول ألأن الوثن شئ أو ان ماذُبح للوثن شئ، بل أن ما يذبحه الأمم إنما يذبحونه للشياطين لا لله، فلست أريد أن تكونوا أنتم شركاء الشياطين، لا تقدرون أن تشربوا كأس الرب وكأس شياطين، ولا تقدرون أن تشتركوا فى مائدة الرب ومائدة شياطين» (١كو ١٠: ١٨-٢١)، ففى هذه الآية يقابل الرسول مائدة الرب أي مذبح المسيحيين بمائدة الأمم ومذبح الشياطين، وبذلك يؤكد إن ما يقدم على مذبح المسيحيين فى سر الشكر الإلهى هو ذبيحة حقيقية أمام الله.

فوائد تناوله:

أما الفوائد التى ينالها المؤمنون بتناولهم من هذا السر باستحقاق فهي كثيرة جداً منها:

1) It binds those who communicate to the Lord intimately, making them one flesh and one spirit with Christ, in accordance with our Savior's words, "He who eats My flesh and drinks My blood abides in Me, and I in him" (Jn 6:56). Through it, the words of the apostle are fulfilled, "for we are members of His body, of His flesh and of His bones" (Eph 5:30), and, "partakers of the divine nature" (2 Pet 1:4).2) His words to them as He handed them the New Covenant saying, "This is My body which is given for you... This cup is... My blood, which is shed for you" (Lk 22:19, 20).

2) Divine fellowship nourishes our bodies and souls, strengthens our faith in the Lord, and advances us in Christian perfection and growth in the spiritual life, as the Lord Christ said, "For My flesh is food indeed, and My blood is drink indeed... As the living Father sent me, and I live because of my Father, so he who feeds on Me will live because of Me" (Jn 6:55,57). The Fathers of the Church teach that the Eucharistic Mystery nourishes the body and soul together; it strengthens them, gives them life, heals them of every weakness, raises them from sin, sanctifies them, purifies from all filthiness, and makes them immoveable and undefeatable in their spiritual struggle for piety, righteousness, and goodness.

3) Divine fellowship serves as a token to our forthcoming resurrection and eternal bliss, as our Savior said, "Whoever eats My flesh and drinks My blood has eternal life, and I will raise him up at the last day" (Jn 6:54), and "If anyone eats of this bread, he will live forever" (Jn 6:51). Ultimately, it is remedy against death, and steadfastness in eternal life through Jesus Christ. Our bodies, after partaking of the Divine Mystery are no longer corruptible, but have the hope of resurrection to eternal life.

أولاً: أنها تربط المشتركين فيه مع الرب إرتباطاً وطيداً، وتُصيرهم جسداً واحداً وروحاً واحداً فى المسيح طبقاً لقول مخلصنا له المجد «من يأكل جسدى ويشرب دمى يثبت فى وأنا فيه»(يو٦: ٥٦). فاذاً به يتم قول الرسول «نصير أعضاء جسمه من لحمه ومن عظامه» (أف ٥: ٣٠) ونصير شركاء الطبيعة الالهية (٢بط ١: ٤).

ثانياً: إن الشركة الالهية تُغذى أجسادنا ونفوسنا، وتوطد إيماننا فى الرب، وتقدمنا فى الكمال المسيحى والنمو فى الحياة الروحية، كما قال السيد المسيح «لأن جسدي مأكل حق ودمى مشرب حق.. كما أرسلنى الآب الحى وأنا حىّ بالآب فمن يأكلنى يحيا بى» (يو٦: ٥٥، ٥٧).يُعلّم آباء الكنيسة بأن سر الشكر هو يُغذى الروح والجسد معاً، ويقويهما ويحييهما ويشفيهما من كل ضعف، ويقيمهما من الخطايا، و يقدسهما ويُطهرهما من كل دنس، ويجعلهما غير متزعزعين ولا مغلوبين فى جهادهما الروحى فى سبيل التقوى والبر والصلاح.

ثالثاً: تكون الشركة الالهية بمثابة عربون لقيامتنا المستقبلية وللغبطة الأبدية، كما قال مخلصنا «من يأكل جسدى ويشرب دمي فله حياة أبدية وأنا أقيمه فى اليوم الاخير» (يو٦: ٥٤). وأيضاً «إن أكل أحد من هذا الخبز يحيا إلى الأبد» (يو٦: ٥١). وقد قال الآباء القديسون أيضاً عن سر الشكر إنه دواء لعدم الموت، وتثبيت للحيوة الأبدية بيسوع المسيح، وأن أجسادنا بعد إشتراكها بالسر الإلهى لا تبقى فاسدة، بل تكون لها رجاء القيامة للحياة الأبدية.

The Bread and Wine Changing into the body and blood of the Lord Christ: True body and blood

The Protestant reformer, Martin Luther, thought that the bread remains bread, but within it, through faith, is the body of Christ; and the wine remains wine, but within it, through faith, is the blood of Christ. So, we eat bread and drink wine, but by faith, we eat and drink the body and blood of Christ.

Some others thought that the bread is only bread and the wine is only wine, without change or transformation; they are simply an indication of the body and blood of Christ.

The Holy Orthodox Church and all the ancient churches, however, believed that they are Christ's true body and blood, saying that this is the body that He took from the Virgin Mary, was crucified on the cross, and is in heaven. The Church supports and affirms this faith with strong evidence from the Holy Bible, even from the Lord Christ's own words, "the bread that I shall give is My flesh, which I shall give for the life of the world" (Jn 6:51). This is the same bread that He promised and called His body.

Figurative, Illustrative, and Symbolic Errors

If the Master's words, "This is My body... this is My blood," were figurative or symbolic, He would not have said the operative word, "This is My body... this is My blood." This is supported by the words of inspiration by the mouth of St. Paul: "The Lord Jesus on the same night in which He was betrayed took bread; and when He had given thanks, He broke it and said, 'Take, eat; this is My body which is broken for you'" (1 Cor 11: 23–24). This evinces that this Mystery is truly the Lord Christ's body and blood, not simply a commemorative symbol, but authentic, according to His own words, "For My flesh is food indeed, and My blood is drink indeed. He who eats My flesh and drinks My blood abides in Me, and I in him" (Jn 6:55–56).

إستحالة الخبز والخمر إلى جسد ودم السيد المسيح: جسد ودم حقيقيان:

إعتقد لوثيرس (وهو مارتن لوثر مؤسس البروتستانتية) أن الخبز يبقى خبزاً، ولكن داخله بالإيمان جسد السيد المسيح. والخمر يبقى خمراً، ولكن داخله بالايمان دم المسيح، فنأكل ونشرب خبزاً وخمراً ولكن بالإيمان نأكل ونشرب جسد ودم السيد المسيح.

قد اعتقد البعض أن الخبز هو خبز فقط والخمر هو خمر فقط بدون تغير ولا استحالة بل أن ذلك يشير فقط إلى جسد المسيح ودمه.

أما الكنيسة الارثوذكسية المقدسة وجميع الكنائس القديمة تؤمن أنهما جسد المسيح ودمه الحقيقيان. وتقول انه هو الجسد الذي أخذه من مريم العذراء، وهو الذى صلب على الصليب، وهو الذي فى السماء. وتعزز معتقدها هذا وتثبته ببراهن قوية من الكتاب المقدس. ومن قول السيد المسيح نفسه «الخبز الذى أُعطى هو جسدى الذى أبذله لأجل خلاص العالم» (يو٦: ٥١) وهو عين الخبز الذى وعد به هكذا وسماه جسده.

خطأ المجاز والمثال والرمز:

فلو كان قول السيد «هذا هو جسدي وهذا هو دمي» هو قول مَثَلى أو رمزي لما كان يقول تلك الكلمة الفعالة «هذا هو جسدى، وهذا هو دمى» ويؤيد ذلك ما نطق به الوحى على لسان بولس الرسول «إن الرب يسوع في الليلة التى أُسلِمَ فيها، أخذ خبزاً وشكر فكسر وقال خذوا كلوا هذا هو جسدى المكسور لأجلكم» (١كو١١: ٢٣، ٢٤). ولذلك تحقق بأجلي بيان أن هذا السر هو جسد السيد المسيح ودمه وليس هما مجرد تذكار بل هما حقيقيان كقوله -له المجد- «لان جسدى مأكل حق ودمى مشرب حق» (يو٦ : ٥٥)، فهو ليس مجازى «من يأكل جسدى ويشرب دمى يثبت فى وأنا فيه» (يو ٦: ٥٦).

The Apostle Paul demonstrated the importance of this Mystery, and warns those who approach it unworthily: "Therefore whoever eats this bread or drinks this cup of the Lord in an unworthy manner will be guilty of the body and blood of the Lord" (1 Cor 11:27). He continued, "For he who eats and drinks in an unworthy manner eats and drinks judgment to himself, not discerning the Lord's body" (1 Cor 11:29). Is it reasonable for a person to convey such detrimental threats and warnings over eating bread and drinking wine? Would God's justice cast His creation into condemnation, denunciation, and retribution for eating bread and drinking wine? Would God make us equivalent to the deceived, and equate the condemnation of the bread and wine with the condemnation of those who crucified Him? Would God give us a pebble and demand of us a pearl, and equate the value of His precious body and blood with the value of the bread and wine which God made for the sustenance of humans? There are two issues here: either the bread is Christ's pure body, and the wine His precious blood, in this case, the terrible threats and severe warnings are in place; or, the bread remains simply bread and the wine remains simply wine. Does God's justice decree for the faithful to be denounced and suffer the judgment of retribution for simple bread and wine? All the evidence provided shows that it was never mentioned in the Holy Bible that the bread and wine would be a representation, a sign, or a symbol of the holy body and blood of Christ, to whom is due all glory and honor from now and forever. Amen.

وقد برهن الرسول على أهمية هذا السر ويحذر الذين يتقدمون اليه بغير استحقاق قائلاً « أى من أكل هذا الخبز أو شرب كأس الرب بدون استحقاق يكون مجرماً فى جسد الرب ودمه» (١كو ١١: ٢٧). وأردف الكلام قائلا «من يأكل ويشرب بدون استحقاق يأكل ويشرب دينونة لنفسه غير مميز جسد الرب ودمه» (١كو١١: ٢٧-٢٩). وهل من عاقل يقول أن مثل هذه التهديدات والتحذيرات الشديدة هى لاجل أكل خبز وشرب خمر؟ أفعدل الله يقتضى هكذا أن يرمى خليقته في الدينونة والشجب والقصاص لأجل أكل الخبز وشرب خمر. أفيجعلنا الله مساوين للصالبين ويعادل دينونة الخبز والخمر بدينونة من صلبوه؟ وهل يعطينا الله حصاة ويطالبنا بلؤلؤة، ويعادل قيمة جسده ودمه الكريمين بقيمة الخبز والخمر اللذين جعلهما الله قوتاً للإنسان. فالمسألة صارت تحت أمرين أما أن يكون الخبز جسد المسيح الطاهر والخمر دمه الكريم. وحينذاك يكون موقع التهديدات الرهيبة والتحذيرات الشديدة فى محلها. وأما أن يكون الخبز لم يزل خبزاً والخمر خمراً على بساطتهما. فعدل الله لا يقتضى أن يشجب مؤمنيه ويوقعهم فى دينونة القصاص لأجل خبز وخمر بسيطين، فمما تقدم عن البراهين التى أوردناها تبين لنا أنه لم يَرد مطلقاً فى الكتاب المقدس أن الخبز والخمر يكونان إشارة أو علامة أو رمز على جسد ودم المسيح الاقدسين الذى له المجد والكرامة من الآن والى الأبد أمين.

HOLY GREAT FRIDAY

بيان يوم الجمعة العظيمة من البصخة المقدسة

Brook Kidron

After our Savior ate the Passover with His disciples in Jerusalem, they praised while journeying to Mount Olivet beyond Brook Kidron (Cf. Jn 18:1). This deep brook, also named the Black Brook, is located between Jerusalem and Mount Olivet. Its stream starts about one and a half miles northwest of Jerusalem and flows southeast until it reaches the northeastern corner of the city wall, at which point, it then streams east of the city. It claims the name Valley of Jehoshaphat (Cf. Joel 3:2) when the city wall is to its west, and Mount Olivet and the Hill of Disobedience are to its east; then, it stretches toward Mar Saba where it bears the name Monk Valley. From there, it extends to Lot's sea, where it bears the name Fire Creek; it is also known as Cedar (Cedron) Valley. After the obscene image of Maachah (Cf. 1 Kg 15:13; 2 Chr 15:16) was burned, and all the vain worship utensils which

وادى قدرون:

بعد ما أكل مخلصنا -له المجد- الفصح مع تلاميذه بأورشليم، سبحوا وخرجوا إلى جبل الزيتون الى عبر وادى قدرون (يو ١٨: ١)، وكان هذا الوادى عميقاً، ويسمى بالوادي الأسود. وكان موقعه بين أورشليم وجبل الزيتون. يبتدئ على بعد ميل ونصف الى الشمال الغربي من أورشليم ويسير الى الجنوب الشرقى الى أن يصل الي زاوية السور الشمالية الشرقية، ثم ينحدر شرقى المدينة. ويسمي وادى قدرون أيضاً «وادى يهوشافاط» (يؤ ٣: ٢)، وهو بين سور المدينة من الجانب الغربي وجبل الزيتون وتل المعصية من الجانب الشرقى، ثم ينحدر الى «مار سابا» حيث يسمى «وادى الراهب». ومن ثم يمتد إلى بحر لوط وهناك يسمي «وادى النار». ويسمى

profaned the Lord's temple were cast into this brook (Cf. 2 Chr 29:16; 30:14; 2 Kg 23:4, 6, 12), this brook became a common cemetery (Cf. 2 Kg 23:6). David crossed this brook when he fled from his son Absalom (Cf. 2 Sam 15:23, 30); likewise, the Lord Christ while in Gethsemane (aware that Judas was familiar with this place) did not attempt to hide. Rather, He was prepared to propitiate Himself for the sins of the world, to the extent that He did not wait for the soldiers to inquire of Him. In anticipation, He went out to meet them, asking, "Whom are you seeking?" (Jn 18:4). This was at midnight on Friday, the 15th day of the month of Nisan.

The High Priests Judge the Lord Christ

The High Priest's Court

The soldiers arrested the Savior; the disciples seeing their teacher bound and led away, forsook Him and fled. But two of them (Peter and John) calmed their fears and followed the multitude to the court of the high priest, Annas (father-in-law of Caiaphas). Customarily, members of this council assembled in one of the temple quarters, but they were also permitted to meet at the high priest's court. Perhaps, the intended purpose of this meeting was to conceal their conspiracy from the multitude, especially since at that time, the temple quarters were overcrowded with people during the Passover.

The High Priesthood

As for the occupation of the high priest, the first to assume it was Aaron (Ex 29), and in the first centuries of Israelite history, the eldest descendent was to inherit it (Num 3:10). However with the conquest of the Greek

أيضاً «بوادى الأرز»، وفي هذا الوادى أُحرقت تماثيل معكة (١مل١٥: ١٣)، (٢أخ١٥: ١٦)، وطرحت جميع أدوات العبادة الباطلة التى تَنجس بها هيكل الرب (٢أخ٢٩: ١٦)، (٣٠: ١٤)، (٢مل٢٣: ٤،٦،١٢)، ثم صار ذلك الوادى مكاناً للمقابر (٢مل ٢٣: ٦). ومم يُذكر أنه عبر هذا الوادى هرب داود من وجه إبنه ابشالوم (٢صم١٥: ٢٣،٣٠)، ويذكر أيضاً أن السيد المسيح عندما ذهب الى جثسيمانى وهو عالم أن يهوذا كان يعرف هذا المكان لم يرد أن يختفى بعد، بل كان مستعداً أن يقدم ذاته كفارة عن خطايا العالم، حتى أنه لم ينتظر الجند ليسألوا من هو، بل سبقهم وخرج لإستقبالهم وسألهم «من تطلبون؟» (يو١٨: ٤)، وكان ذلك في نصف الليل من ليلة الجمعة الموافقة خمسة عشر نيسان.

محاكمة رؤساء الكهنة للسيد المسيح له المجد

دار رئيس الكهنة:

لما قبض الجند على المخلص -له المجد- ورأى التلاميذ أن معلمهم قد أُوثِقَ وأُخِذَ فتركوه وهربوا، غير أن إثنين منهم سَكن روعهما وهما بطرس ويوحنا اللذان تبعا الجمع إلى دار رئيس الكهنة «حنان» الذى كان حما «قيافا»، وكان من عادة أعضاء ذلك المجلس أن يجتمعوا فى إحدى ديارات الهيكل، وكان يجوز لهم الإجتماع فى دار رئيس الكهنة. ولعل غاية إجتماعهم هذا إخفاء مشورتهم عن الشعب، لأن ديار الهيكل كانت فى ذلك الوقت غاصة بالناس لأنها كانت أيام الفصح.

وظيفة رئيس الكهنة:

وأما عن وظيفة رئيس الكهنة فكان أول من تولاها هو «هرون» (خر ٢٩)، وكان يرثها الأكبر من سلالته (عد٣: ١٠) فى القرون الأولى من تاريخ الاسرائيليين ولما إستولى ملوك

empire, this occupation was sold to anyone paying a substantial amount. Thereafter, with the Roman conquest, the high priest was appointed and discharged according to the empire's fancy, irrespective of the lineage or qualification of the person. This detestable habit continued from the time of Herod the Great, until the devastation of Jerusalem.

Annas was a very prominent and influential figure, and so managed to attain the position of high priesthood, not only for himself, but also for his son Eleazar, his son-in-law Caiaphas, and four more sons. Each one who held this position was given the title of high priest and sat at the great assembly for the duration of his life, even if deposed.

Such was the case with Annas; he retained his title as high priest, although he had been deposed from this position four years before the crucifixion. His name preceded that of Caiaphas because he was older in age and more tenured and experienced in the position. When the Jews arrested the Lord Christ, they first took Him to Annas, to enlist his approval and endorsement of the arrest, and then, they took the Lord of glory bound to Caiaphas (Jn 18:24).

Caiaphas

Joseph, also known as Caiaphas (according to Josephus the historian), was present at the time when the judgment to crucify the Lord Christ was passed (Jn 11:49–61). Being a member of the Sadducees sect, and Annas' son-in-law, he was also spuriously given the title of high priest (Jn 11:49). Caiaphas is the one who said, "It is expedient for us that one man should die for the people, and not that the whole nation should perish" (Jn 11:49–50). Just as the case with Annas, Caiaphas, too, was deposed as the high priest at the will of the Romans. He was deposed by Vitalious (or Valarius), Pontius Pilate's successor, as the Roman governor ruling Judea. This occurred six years after the Lord Christ's crucifixion.

اليونـان عـلى الإسرائيليـين صـاروا يبيعـون لهـم تلـك الوظيفـة لمـن يدفـع فيهـا ثمنـاً وافـراً، وبعـد أن إسـتولى عليهـم الرومانيـون أخـذوا يعزلـون الرئيـس ويقيمـون غـيره كـما يريـدون، غـير مراعـين أهليـة ومقـدرة الشـخص المرغـوب فيـه. وإسـتمرت هـذه العـادة الممقوتـة مـن عـصر «هـيرودس الكبـير» الى زمـان خـراب أورشـليم.

ويظهـر أن «حنـان» كان ذا سـطوة قويـة وجـاه عظيـم حتـى إنـه حصـل عـلى رئاسـة الكهنـوت ليـس لإبنـه «اليعـازر» وصهـره «قيافـا» فحسـب، بـل بالأكـثر لأربعـة آخريـن مـن بنيـه، وكان يلقـب كل مـن أخـذ تلـك الوظيفـة برئيـس الكهنـة ويجلـس فى المجلـس الكبـير طـوال أيـام حياتـه حتـى ولـو عُـزِلَ.

وهكـذا جـرى مـع حنـان فإنـه دُعـى رئيـس الكهنـة مـع أنـه كان معـزولاً مـن وظيفتـه وقتئـذ [قبـل الصلـب بأربعـة سـنوات]. وقُـدِمَ إسـمه عـلي إسـم قيافـا لأنـه أكـبر منـه سـناً وأقـدم فى الوظيفـة ولـه خـبرة واسـعة، ولمـا أمسـك اليهـود السـيد المسـيح لـه المجـد قدمـوه أولا إلى «حنـان» إسـتجلاباً لمصادقتـه وإرضائـه عـما فعلـوا، ومـن ثـم أخـذوا السـيد لـه المجـد موثقـاً إلى «قيافـا» (يـو ١٨: ٢٤).

قيافا:

«قيافـا» إسـمه «يوسـف» كـما ذكـر يوسـيفوس المـؤرخ، وقـد كان حـاضراً وقـت القضـاء عـلي السـيد المسـيح بالصلـب (يـو١١: ٤٩-٦١)، وكان صدوقـى المذهـب وكان صهـر «حنـان» و»كان رئيسـاً للكهنـة فى تلـك السـنة» (يـو١١: ٤٩)، وهـو الـذى قـال: «خـير لنـا أن يمـوت واحـد عـن الشـعب ولا تهلـك الأمـة كلهـا» (يـو١١: ٤٩-٥٠)، ولأن الدولـة الرومانيـة فى ذاك الوقـت كانـت تنصـب رئيـس الكهنـة أو تعزلـه حسـب إرادتهـا، لذلـك كـما حـدث مـع حنـان الـذى عُـزل مـن رومـا كرئيـس كهنـة، هكـذا قيافـا أيضـاً عزلـه فيتاليـوس أو فالوريـوس سـلف بيلاطـس فى الحكومـة اليهوديـة وهـو القائـد الرومـانى، وكان ذلـك بعـد سـتة سـنوات مـن صلـب السـيد المسـيح لـه المجـد.

Condemning the Savior at Night

The Sanhedrin assembled, and called an unofficial preliminary session. This took place when Annas sent Jesus to Caiaphas (shortly after midnight), where our Savior was first examined. He remained alone before Caiaphas and the council members, who mocked Him until almost dawn, or the time of the cock's crowing (during which time, Peter denied the Lord Christ three times).

As Friday morning neared, the great council convened in the temple to uphold the ruling of the previous unofficial session that took place during the night in the high priest's court. The ruling deliberated was the death of Jesus. This was considered merely an expression of the members' opinions because it contradicted both Jewish law, which prohibits conducting an examination during the night, and also Roman law, which forbids passing a ruling before dawn. This reveals the intensity of the high priests' wrath towards Jesus, and their dread of His impact on the people. The council met at night in order to fabricate an accusation for His death.

The high priest deceptively asked Jesus, "I put You under oath by the living God: Tell us if You are the Christ, the Son of God!" (Mt 26:63; Mk 14:61). At Jesus' reply, Caiaphas displayed disgust and shock, declaring Him blasphemous, and therefore, he needed no further witnesses to rule against Him. They took a unanimous judgment that His punishment is death (Jn 19:7; Mk 14:64), although neither they nor their rulers had authority to carry out such a conviction.

Thus, they took Jesus to Pilate, the Roman governor, to condemn Christ to be crucified. It is no secret that the great council alone had a lawful right to deliberate on criminal cases and assign its penalty. They had no authority to pass a judgment of death upon anyone, for the Roman authority had suspended this right many years earlier.

The chief priest tore his clothes (Mt 26:65), a universal sign of mourning for Jews (2 Kg 18:37; 19:1; Esth 4:1), intending by this to show his disgust at the extent of the blasphemy in his presence. He testified that Jesus was a

محاكمة المخلص ليلاً:

إجتمع أعضاء مجمع السبعين وعقدوا جلسة إستعدادية غير رسمية. ولابد أن يكون مخلصنا قد فُحص أولا أمام «قيافا» لما أرسله اليه «حنان» بعد منتصف الليل بقليل، وبقى مخلصنا له المجد أمام قيافا وحده، وأمام أعضاء المجمع إلى قرب الفجر يستهزئون به الى وقت صياح الديك، وهنا أنكر بطرس السيد المسيح ثلاث مرات.

لما كان نهار صباح يوم الجمعة إجتمع المجمع الكبير فى الهيكل وأثبت حكم الجلسة السابقة الغير الرسمية والتى عُقِدت فى الليل فى دار رئيس الكهنة، لأن الحكم علي يسوع بالموت فى تلك الجلسة كان يُعتبر كمجرد تصريح برأى الأعضاء، لأنه كان مخالفاً لشريعة اليهود أن يُجري فحص جناية فى الليل، وكذلك مخالفاً للشريعة الرومانية أن يصدر حكم قبل الفجر. ويَظهر من ذلك أن غضب رؤساء الكهنة كان شديداً على يسوع له المجد، وإنهم كانوا خائفين جداً من تأثير أقواله فى الشعب، لذلك إجتمعوا فى الليل لكى يخترعوا عليه تهماً ملفقة لإماتته.

حينئذ سأله رئيس الكهنة «أستحلفك بالله الحى أن تقول لنا هل أنت هو المسيح إبن الله» (مت ٢٦: ٦٣)، (مر١٤: ٦١) فلما أجاب يسوع على السؤال، تظاهر قيافا بالاشمئزاز من جوابه، وحسبه تجديفاً، وقال أنه غير محتاج إلى شهود بعد، فحكموا عليه بالإجماع بالموت (يو١٩: ٧)، (مر ١٤: ٦٤)، غير أنه لم يكن لهم ولا لرؤسائهم قوة تنفيذ هذا الحكم.

لذلك أخذوا يسوع إلى بيلاطس الحاكم الرومانى لكي يأمر بصلبه. وليس بالأمر الخفى أن المجمع الكبير كان له وحده الحق الشرعى فى الحكم على الدعاوى الجنائية التى تستوجب القصاص، إلا إنه لم يكن له سلطاناً فى ذلك الوقت أن يُجرى الحكم بالموت على أحد، لأن الحكومة الرومانية كانت قد نَزعت منه ذلك السلطان قبل هذا الوقت بعدة سنين.

ولما حدث أن رئيس الكهنة مزق ثيابه (مت٢٦: ٦٥)، وكانت هذه هى العلامة

blasphemer, and incited the council to concur with his ruling against Him. His entire emotional enactment was a hypocritical and deceptive attempt to promote his evil objective. He further added to his iniquity by tearing his clothes, because according to Mosaic Law, the chief priest was forbidden from tearing his clothes (Lev 10:6; 21:10). From that point forward, the priesthood was torn away from the Jewish nation.

It was the council members' duty to impartially investigate if what the Lord of glory said was true or not. Instead, they hardened their hearts from hearing the truth and condemned Him, in accordance with Mosaic Law for blasphemers, to be subject to stoning (Cf. Jn 10:31; Lev 24:16).[36]

The council members had two options, they either could have ordered the people to stone Jesus (disregarding the Roman decree, as they later did in the case of Stephen), or they could have obtained authorization from Pilate. They refrained from the latter, in fear that many from the crowd would come to defend Jesus and rescue Him. They resorted to ask Pilate to carry out their charge to kill Jesus. At that time, Roman law passed judgment of crucifixion in cases of blasphemy. This was the Lord of glory's accusation, and thus, He was to die in the flesh—crucified, and not stoned. These council members were in agreement on their judgment, yet in order to make it lawful, because according to their assembly by-laws it was forbidden to carry out nocturnal judgments against criminals, they had to meet again. Therefore, they met once more after the break of dawn and repeated the charge against Him (Mt 27:3) (this was the last time Jesus stood before the Jewish rulers).

المألوفة للحزن عند اليهود (٢مل١٨: ٣٧، ١٩: ١)، (أس ٤: ١)، وكان قد قصد رئيس الكهنة بها أن يُظهر إشمئزازه من فظاعة التجديف، ولكى تكون شهادة علي يسوع -له المجد- بأنه جدف، وحضاً للمجلس بالحُكْم على يسوع كما حَكَمَ هو عليه، إلا أنه كان كل ما أظهره من الإنفعالات رياءً وخداعاً للوصول فقط إلي تتميم بغيته الشريرة، بينما فِعْل رئيس الكهنة هذا أى تمزيقه لثيابه قد زاد من إثمه، لأنه على موجب شريعة موسى كان لايجوز لرئيس الكهنة أن يمزق ثيابه (لا ١٠: ٦، ٢١: ١٠)، ومن ذلك الحين نُزِعَت من الأمة اليهودية وظيفة الكهنوت.

وكان على أعضاء المجلس أن ينظروا فى الدعوى الموجهة ضده ليعلموا أحق هو كل ما قاله السيد له المجد أم لا، ولكنهم صرفوا أذهانهم عن سماع الحقيقة وقرروا تنفيذ الحكم فيه بالموت رجماً على مقتضي شريعة موسى التى أمرت برجم المجدف[٣٦] (يو ١٠: ٣١)، (لا٢٤: ١٦).

وكان ممكناً لأعضاء المجلس أن يأمروا الناس برجم يسوع على رغم وجود الحكام الرومان كما فعلوا بعد ذلك باستفانوس، وأن يستأذنوا بيلاطس فى ذلك، ولكنهم لم يفعلوا هذا خوفاً من أن كثيرين من الشعب قد يدافعون عن يسوع وينقذونه من أيديهم، فإستحسنوا أن يسألوا بيلاطس أن يُجرى حكمهم، أى أن يقتله. و كان القانون عند الرومانيين يقضى فى مثل هذه الحالات على المجدف بالموت صلباً، وهذه هى علة إختيار السيد له المجد أن يموت بالجسد صلباً لا رجماً. وكان أعضاء ذلك المجمع يعتبرون حكمهم نهائياً، لكنهم إضطُروا أن يجتمعوا أيضاً ليجعلوا هذا الحكم شرعياً، لأنه ممنوع تنفيذ الأحكام التى يصدرونها على المذنبين بالليل حسب قوانين مجلسهم كما ذكرنا قبلاً، فإجتمعوا هذه المرة الثانية بعد طلوع الفجر وكرروا الحكم عليه وأدانوه (مت ٢٧: ٣)، وهذه كانت آخر مرة نُظِرت فيها الدعوى على يسوع أمام قضاة اليهود.

Court Ruling in the Morning

On Friday morning, all the chief priests and elders of the people conspired against Jesus to kill Him. The intention of this session was to affirm the decision taken at the nocturnal meeting, which was contrary to regulations and deemed unlawful according to the Talmud (one of the holiest Jewish books). According to the standards set out in the Talmud, the counsel is prohibited to examine criminal cases at night, especially ones that carry the death penalty. It is necessary for the conviction of death to be passed at the time of trial, and no ruling was to be delivered without self-testimony. Since the counsel broke this fundamental law by trying Jesus at night, they found it necessary to rectify the situation by holding a formal lawful session early in the morning. This session was held in its formal location (in the temple), unlike the nocturnal session, which was held in the court of the high priest. The intended purpose was to question Jesus, and provoke Him to speak blasphemously, in order to procure Pilate's (the Roman governor) collaboration with their sentence. As all the evangelists recorded, they arrested Him and took Him to Pilate (Mt 27:11-30; Mk 15:6-20; Lk 23:13-32; Jn 19:6-7).

Judas' Suicide

When Judas realized He was condemned, he was remorseful and returned the thirty pieces of silver (Mt 27:3). His remorse, however, was not a true repentance; otherwise; he would have sought and attained forgiveness. True repentance leads the transgressor to Christ; yet, this remorse was not from a heart void of deceit. A true repented heart leads to life, but false repentance leads to more transgression. We see this in the example of Judas, who furthered his betrayal by committing suicide. His remorse is likened to Cain and King Saul's, spiraling downward to hopelessness and despair. When Judas' conscience awoke, he felt the gravity of the crime he committed against his good Master—he had relinquished himself to the devil, who in turn, used him to fulfill his evil intentions and left him

جلسة المجمع صباحاً:

ولما كان الصباح أى صباح يوم الجمعة، تشاور جميع رؤساء الكهنة وشيوخ الشعب على يسوع حتى يقتلوه، وكان الغرض من إنعقاد هذه الجلسة إثبات ما حكموا به فى إجتماعهم فى الليل. وكان ذلك على خلاف النظام، كما إنه لم يكن شرعياً حسب نص كتاب التلمود الذى هو من أقدس كتب اليهود، لأنه بموجب ذلك الكتاب لم يجُز للمجلس أن يفحص ليلاً دعاوى جنائية يمكن أن يُحكم فيها على من تثبت عليه بالموت، وكان من المُحتم أن يحكم على المدعى عليه بالموت فى ذات الوقت الذى يُحاكم فيه، وألا ينفذ عليه الحكم إلا بمجرد إقراره على نفسه. وبما إنهم كسروا الشريعة التى تنهى عن الحكم فى القضايا الجنائية فى الليل، رأوا أنه من الواجب أن يعقدوا جلسة رسمية شرعية فى الصباح مبكرين فى ذلك بقدر إمكانهم. وعُقدت هذه الجلسة طبعاً فى المكان الرسمى فى الهيكل، وليست كالجلسة التى عُقدت بالليل فى بيت رئيس الكهنة. وكان المقصود منها إستجواب يسوع وإستماع أقواله، والمشورة بكيفية إجراء توقيع الحكم عليه الذى يقتضى التصديق عليه من بيلاطس الوالى الرومانى كما تقدم، فأوثقوه وأتوا به إلى بيلاطس كما ينص جميع البشيرين (مت٢٧: ١١-٣٠)، (مر١٥: ٦-٢٠)، (لو٢٣: ١٣-٣٢)، (يو١٩: ٦-٧).

إنتحار يهوذا:

حينئذ لما رأي يهوذا أنه قد دين، ندم ورد الثلاثين من الفضة (مت ٢٧: ٣)، فندمه هذا لم يكن توبة حقيقية وإلا لحمله على طلب المغفرة فينالها. فالتوبة الصحيحة تقود المذنب الى المسيح، ولكن هذه الندامة لم تكن صادرة عن قلب نقى من الغش، لأن التوبة الحقيقية تقود الى الحياة وأما التوبة الغير حقيقية فتقود الى زيادة الإثم كما هو مشاهد فى قصة يهوذا. فإنه زاد على خيانته قتله لنفسه، وكان ندمه كندم قايين وشاول الملك ملتجئاً الى اليأس والقنوط. وذاك عندما أنبه ضميره وشعر بعظم الجرم الذى إرتكبه فى حق معلمه الصالح، أسلم نفسه للشيطان فإتخذه إبليس آلة فى يده لإتمام مقاصده الشريرة، ثم تركه بلا تعزية ولا رجاء، ومن ثم تخلت عنه

without consolation or hope. Furthermore, divine help forsook him, and so in despair, he went and hanged himself, adding to his transgressions.

Peter's Remorse

There is a great difference between Judas' remorse, and Peter's remorse. When Peter felt the gravity of his sin, he withdrew from people, sought isolation, and wept bitterly (Lk 22:62) (as the Holy Bible mentions). He did this because of his great shame and sorrow, and for his shortcomings toward the Savior, and for his weakness, fearfulness, blaspheming of grace, and his transgression in denying Christ by cursing and swearing after boasting of his courage and steadfastness. Truth be told, his transgression was very great because he committed it after having spent three years as a disciple of Jesus: hearing His teachings, witnessing His miracles, seeing His signs, and being chosen over the others as one of the three distinguished disciples. He had dined with Him only a few hours earlier, heard His warning, and vowed saying, "If I have to die with You, I will not deny You!" (Mk 14:31). The trials that set Peter to deny Christ were meager, as he was not threatened by great men, strong forces, or the most distinguished of people, but rather by a maidservant. Peter saw John, who "was known to them as one of Christ's disciples" (Jn 18:15–16). Therefore, it cannot be said that Peter's transgression is less than Judas'. But unlike Judas, Peter offered a true repentance. His remorse was not akin to Judas' remorse because Judas' remorse was that of hopelessness, while Peter's remorse led him to seek true repentance. This was exemplified by his isolation, the extent of his remorse, and his regret. His repentance can be likened to David's repentance. The difference between a hypocrite and a Christian is that the first falls and does not rise, while the latter falls but rises remorsefully, penitently, humbly, and consequentially renewed in his spiritual life.

المعونـة الإلهيـة فذهـب وخنـق نفسـه وبذلـك تضاعـف جرمـه.

ندامة بطرس:

فيوجـد فـرق عظيـم مـا بـين ندامـة يهـوذا وندامـة بطـرس، فبطـرس لما شـعر بعظـم الخطـأ الـذى وقـع فيـه إعتـزل النـاس وأحـب الإنفـراد وبـكى بـكاء مـراً (لـو٢٢: ٦٢) كـما يذكـر الكتـاب، لخجلـه وأسـفه الشـديدين عـلى مـا فـرط منـه فى حـق المخلـص وعـلى مـا كان عليـه مـن ضعـف وخـوف وكفـر بالنعمـة، وعـلى إثمـه بأنـه أنكـر المسـيح بحلـف ولعـن بعـد أن كان يفتخـر بشـجاعته وثباتـه، والحـق أن إثمـه كان عظيـماً جـداً، لأنـه إرتكبـه بعـد أن كان تلميـذ ليسـوع ثـلاث سـنوات، وبعـد أن سـمع تعاليمـه وشـاهد معجزاتـه ورأى آياتـه، وكان واحـداً مـن الرسـل الثـلاث المختصـين عـلى غيرهـم، وكان قـد تعـشى معـه قبلهـا ببضـع سـاعات وسـمع تحذيـره لـه مـن هـذا الإثـم، ووعـد بطـرس معلمـه قائـلاً ولـو مـت معـك لا أنكـرك (مـر ١٤: ٣١)، وكانـت دواعـي هـذا الإنـكار قليلـة إذا لم يُهَـدَدْ مـن أكـبر الرجـال ولا مـن أعظـم القـواد ولا مـن أشرف النـاس بـل مـن جاريـة خادمـة، بينـما كان يشـاهد هنـاك يوحنـا يتبـع معلمـه إذ إنـه كان معروفـاً عندهـم أيضـاً إنـه مـن تلاميـذ السـيد المسـيح (يـو١٨: ١٥-١٦)، فكانـت خطيـة بطـرس أقـل تجـاوزاً مـن خطيـة يهـوذا، ولكنـه نـدم عـلى مـا فـرط منـه بندامـة حقيقيـة. ولم يكـن أسـفه كأسـف يهـوذا، لأن أسـف يهـوذا كان أسـف اليـأس بينـما أسـف بطـرس كان أسـف التوبـة الحقيقيـة، والدليـل عـلى هـذا إنفـراده وشـدة ندمـه ودوام تأثـيره فكانـت توبتـه كتوبـة داود النبـى، فالفـرق بـين المـرائى والمسـيحى أن الأول يسـقط ولا يقـوم والثـانى يسـقط ويقـوم نادمـاً تائبـاً متواضعـاً متجـدداً فى الحيـاة الروحيـة.

Jesus before Pilate

When the Savior was sent to the Roman ruler, Pontius Pilate, He was accompanied by the entire great assembly (Lk 23:1; Mt 27:1–2). The intent behind gathering the entire assembly and parading in the morning to Pilates' court was to sway Pilate and convince him that the accused—Jesus, had committed the greatest, most despicable, repugnant crime. When Pilate was informed that the great council members had arrived with a transgressor, they sent Jesus to Pilate and stood at the doorway (they could not enter into the Praetorium because the law forbade them from entering a house where there is leaven). They did not enter lest they become unclean and are prohibited from eating the Passover. Knowing this, Pilate went out to meet them. They were eager to present their accuser, without mentioning the reasons for which the great assembly had condemned Him, in hopes to establish a hasty conviction. However, their hope was lost when Pilate asked, "What accusation do you bring against this Man?" (Jn18:29). At this point, they were compelled to declare their fabricated accusation. After hearing this, Pilate declared that he found no reason for convicting Jesus to death (Lk 23:22,14,4; Jn 18:38, 19:6,4), which disenchanted their hopes to condemn Christ. St. Luke the Evangelist mentions that Pilate publicly confessed trice that he found no justifiable reason for our Savior's death; he further confessed that Herod also found no reason (Lk 23:14-15).

Pilate

Pilate was also known as Pontius. Archelaus, the son of Herod the Great, was the last king over Judea.(he was removed from ruling in the year 6 AD). From that time forward, Caesar appointed governors over Judea. Pilate was Tiberius Caesar's sixth appointed governor over Judea. He governed Judea for ten years (six before Christ's crucifixion, and four after His Resurrection). He was known to be ruthless, unjust, temperamental, and sought only his personal gain; he did not care for the good of others. The Jews rebelled against his reign often. Consequently, he shed their blood readily to suffocate their insurrections, so much so that the Jews

يسوع أمام بيلاطس:

ولما أُرسل المخلص له المجد فى المرة الأولى إلى الوالى الرومانى صحبه كل المجمع الكبير (مت ٢٧: ١-٢)، (لو٢٣: ١)، ولابد أنهم كانوا يقصدون من تجمهرهم هذا والذهاب بموكب حافل من ادنياء وكبراء أن يموهوا على عقل بيلاطس ويقنعوه بأن يسوع قد إرتكب جناية من أفظع وأشنع الجنايات التى لم يُسمع بمثلها، مبالغين فى إستدانته. ولما أُخبِرَ بيلاطس بأن أعضاء المجلس الكبير أتوه بمذنب، وانهم لا يقدرون أن يدخلوا إلى الوالى فى دار الولاية [تبعاً للقانون الذى يحرم عليهم دخول بيوت فيها خمير] فدفعوا بيسوع إلى بيلاطس، وهم لبثوا بإزاء الباب فى الطريق، ولم يدخلوا لئلا يتنجسوا فيمتنعوا من أكل الفصح إنما خرج هو لمقابلتهم. ولا ريب أنهم كانوا يطمعون فى إثبات حكمهم حالاً بدون ذِكر الأسباب التى دانه عليها المجمع الكبير. غير أنه قد خاب أملهم عند سؤال بيلاطس لهم «أية شكاية تقدمون على هذا الانسان؟» (يو١٨: ٢٩) فاضطروا إلى أن يقرروا الذنب الموهوم. وأسفرت النتيجة عن أن بيلاطس أعلن أنه لم يجد فيه علة يستوجب عليها الموت (لو٢٣: ٤، ١٤، ٢٢) ، (يو١٨: ٣٨، ١٩: ٤،٦)، [هنا ويذكر معلمنا لوقا البشير أن بيلاطس إعترف وأعلن ثلاث مرات إنه لم يجد فى مخلصنا علة للموت، بل وبالأكثر إعترافه أن هيرودس أيضاً لم يجد فيه علة للموت (لو٢٣: ١٤-١٥)].

بيلاطس:

بيلاطس هذا كان يلقب بالبنطى، كان أرخلاوس بن هيرودس الكبير آخر ملك علي اليهودية وكان قد نفى من حكمه سنة ست للميلاد، ومن ذلك الوقت أخذ قيصر يقيم على اليهودية الولاة، فكان بيلاطس سادس والي على اليهودية عينه طيباريوس قيصر، وكان قد تولى اليهودية مدة عشرة سنوات (ستاً منهم قبل صلب السيد المسيح وأربعاً بعد قيامته). وكان قاسياً ظالماً سريع التقلب لا يسعي الا لمنافعه الشخصية ولا يكترث بمصالح الاخرين، وكثيراً ما عصاه اليهود، فسفك دماء كثيرين منهم اخماداً لفتنهم، فأبغضوه أشد البغض وشكوه عدت مرات لقيصر.

passionately despised him and complained to Caesar several times.

Although he could discern truth and justice, he lacked the courage to avenge the wronged and defend the truth when there was resistance. He hated and abhorred the Jews, but he feared their complaints to the emperor. He was removed from his governorate at the same time that Caiaphas was removed from the priesthood.

The governor's headquarters was in Caesarea, on the Roman seashore (Acts 23:23–33; 25:1,4,6,13). The governor was tasked with traveling to Jerusalem during the great feasts to make rulings and maintain the peace, by preventing troubles and nuisances evidently of large crowds. The governor's house in Jerusalem is in the palace called, Herod's Palace (the Praetorium) on Mount Zion.

Jesus Sent to Herod

As Pilate was debating on how to sidestep judging the Lord Christ, the mention of Galilee, in passing, gave him the idea that he could pass the burden to Herod Antipas, the tetrarch of Galilee (Lk 3:1), who ruled for 42 years (four years before the Lord Christ's crucifixion, and thereafter, the remainder). He was the second son of Herod the Great and from his fourth wife, Miltaki. Like his father before him, he craved glory, and indulged in grandeur and extravagance. He is the one the Master called a fox (Lk 13:32). Also, like his father, he had spent grand sums on community buildings. He built Tiberius in honor of the emperor Tiberius Caesar. When his wife, Herodias, urged him to go to Rome to seek the royal title, Emperor Caligula removed him from his position, and exiled him to Leon in Gaul for his trespasses.

It has been mentioned at least five times that Herod Antipas has taken the wife of his brother Philip [not Philip the Tetrarch], and John the Baptist rebuked him. Although previously he rejoiced at the teachings of John, he eventually beheaded John in prison and handed his head to Salome, the daughter of Herodias, in order to fulfill his promise to her (Mt 14:11; Mk

إلا أنـه كان بصيراً فى بيـان الحـق والعـدل لكنـه لم تكـن لـه القـوة والشـجاعة لينصـف المظلـوم، وليحامـي عـن الحـق عنـد وجـود شـغب ومقاومـة. فـكان بـدوره يكـره اليهـود ويبغضهـم لكنـه كان يخـشى شـكواهم إيـاه للإمبراطـور. وكان قـد عُـزِلَ مـن ولايتـه فى الوقـت الـذى عُـزِلَ فيـه قيافـا مـن كهنوتـه.

كان مركـز الـوالى في قيصريـة عـلي شـاطئ بحـر الـروم (أع ٢٣: ٢٣-٣٣، ٢٥: ١، ٤، ٦، ١٣)، لكنـه كان يذهـب إلى أورشـليم فى أيـام الاعيـاد العظيمـة ليمنـع الشـغب والتشـويش الـذى كان يحـدث مـن الجمـع وليُجـرى الأحـكام. وكان منـزل الـوالى فى أورشـليم فى القـصر الـذي يُسـمى قـصر هـيرودس الكبـير عـلى جبـل صهيـون.

يسوع أُرسل الى هيرودس:

ولمـا كان بيلاطـس حائـراً فى مـاذا يفعـل ليتخلـص مـن إدانتـه للسـيد لـه المجـد و ذكـر أمامـه أن المخلـص مـن الجليـل، خطـر فى بالـه أنـه يمكنـه أن يُخـلى نفسـه مـن هـذه المسـؤولية بإرسـاله إلى هـيرودس انتيبـاس رئيـس الربـع فى الجليـل (لـو٣: ١). هـيرودس هـذا كانـت مـدة وجـوده فى الحكـم هـى أثنـين وأربعـين سـنه (أربعـة منهـا قبـل صلـب السـيد المسـيح والباقـى بعـد صلبـه)، وكان ثـانى أبنـاء هـيرودس الاكـبر مـن إمرأتـه الرابعـة ملثـاكى، وكان مثـل أبيـه راغبـاً فى المجـد والعظمـة ورغـد العيـش، وهـو الـذى سـماه ربنـا ثعلبـاً (لـو١٣: ٣٢)، وقـد أنفـق كابيـه مبالـغ طائلـة في المبـاني العموميـة، فبنـى «طبريـة» إكرامـاً للامبراطـور طيباريـوس قيـصر. حـدث أن حرضتـه إمرأتـه «هيروديـا» بـأن يتوجـه إلى روميـة لـكي يطلـب لقـب ملـك غير أن الامبراطـور «كليكـولا» عذلـه مـن وظيفتـه و نفـاه إلى ليـون فى غاليـا لسـبب ذنوبـه.

وقـد ذُكـر خمـس مـرات عـلى الأقـل أن هـيرودس أنتيبـاس هـذا كان قـد أتخـذ زوجـة فيلبـس أخيـه زوجـة لـه (مـت١٤: ٣)، (مـر٦: ١٧)، (لـو١٣: ١٩) ، وبسـبب هـذا كان يوحنـا المعمـدان يوبخـه بشـدة، بالرغـم مـن إنـه كان سـابقاً يمتـدح تعاليمـه، لكنـه وضعـه في

6:16–28).

Herod was in Jerusalem for the Passover, and thus, also passed judgment against the Lord Christ. Pilate sent Jesus, being a Galilean, to Herod's jurisdiction. Herod was very glad to meet the Savior, because for a long time, he had wanted to see Him. He took this opportunity to ask Him many questions, but the Master refused to answer any of his questions (Lk 23:7–12). Herod begged Him to perform a miracle before his eyes, but again, the Lord with His divine wisdom refrained. In turn, Herod and his men of war mocked Jesus, but He maintained His silence—answering nothing.

Herod considered Pilate's act of sending Jesus to him for judgment as a gesture of respect and honor. This was the cause of reinstating their friendship, which went sour after Pilate killed the Galileans, as mentioned in the Gospel according to St. Luke (Lk 13:1).

Glory to You O Lord, for by Your amazing birth, You brought peace to earth and reconciled us to God Your Father, and at Your death You removed the enmity from the hearts of the kings. Truly, You are the King of reconciliation and peace.

Judgment against Jesus

After Jesus returned from Herod, He was brought again before Pilate. This time, Pilate officially sat on the judgment seat and declared that he had accurately examined Jesus and found not one fault in Him deserving of death, and that Herod had concurred with this same decree. As such, Pilate still insisted on releasing Jesus. He declared he would scourge Him and release Him, hoping this would appease the Jewish nation, especially the priests. This pleased no one, but rather those present shouted loudly, "Crucify this Man and release to us Barabbas!" (Cf. Lk 23:18) (which means son of 'Abbas'). He was infamous for shedding blood and committing offenses. He was cast into prison for his insurrection and rebellion. It is

السجن الى أن أعطى رأسه الى إبنة هيروديا عندما إضطر لإيفاء وعده لها (مت١٤: ١١)، (مر٦: ١٦-٢٨).

وكان هيرودس أحد القضاة عند محاكمة المسيح له المجد لأنه إتفق حضوره إلى أورشليم في ذلك الوقت لعيد الفصح، فأرسل بيلاطس يسوع اليه لانه كان جليلياً تحت سلطانه. أما هيرودس فقبل المخلص بكل فرح لانه كان مشتاقاً من زمن طويل أن يراه. وإذ اشتهى هيرودس أن يعلم عنه شيئاً أخذ يسأله الكثير من الإسئلة لكن السيد المسيح لم يجبه بشئ عما سأله (لو٢٣: ٧-١٢)، وترجاه أن يصنع أمامه آية فلم يصنع، حسبما إقتضت حكمته الالهية، فهزأ به هو وجنوده أما يسوع فبقى ساكتاً ولم يجبه بشئ.

وقد اعتبر هيرودس ارسال يسوع اليه من قبل بيلاطس هى علامة اعتبار ومحبة. وكان ذلك سبب لإرجاع الصداقة بينهما التى كانت قد إنحلت عراها بسبب ذبح بيلاطس للجليليين المذكورين فى لوقا (لو١٣: ١).

المجد لك يا رب فى ميلادك العجيب ألقيت سلاما على الارض وصالحتنا مع الله أبيك، وعند موتك نزعت العداوة من قلوب الملوك، حقاً إنك رئيس الصلح والسلام.

الحكم على يسوع:

بعد رجوع مخلصنا له المجد من عند هيرودس، أُحضر مرة ثانية أمام بيلاطس الذى كان لم يزل مصمماً على إطلاقه. ثم جلس فى هذه المرة على كرسى القضاء رسيماً وأعلن انه قد فحص يسوع فحصاً دقيقاً فلم يجد فيه علة واحدة تستوجب الموت، وقد أقر أيضاً هيروس هذا الاقرار ولذلك قال انه سيؤدبه ويطلقه، آملا بذلك أنه يرضى أمة اليهود وخصوصاً الكهنة. غير إنه لم يرض أحداً منهم بل إرتفع صراخ الموجودين أصلب لنا هذا وأطلق باراباس (لو٢٣: ١٨). ومعنى إسم باراباس هو ابن عباس، وهو رجل كان قد اشتهر بسفك الدماء وارتكابه المعاصى، وكان ملقى فى السجن بتهمة

probable that he was from the faction that abhorred Roman authority, and had set the city in an uproar with his rebellion and murderous ways.

Ironically, Barabbas was guilty of the exact charge the chief priests falsely laid on the Savior—rebellion. No greater or clearer evidence could be presented, only the demise of the Pharisees and their supports in the hypocritical scheme to fiercely ask the Roman ruler to release the transgressor, Barabbas, and condemn the righteous Savior. "When Pilate saw that he could not prevail at all, but rather that a tumult was rising, he took water and washed his hands before the multitude, saying, 'I am innocent of the blood of this just Person. You see to it'" (Mt 27:24; Duet 21:6–9). These words did not acquit Pilate. Although, he did truly wash his hands with water, yet this did not wash his heart from transgression—he did deliver to death One whom he had judged as innocent, simply because the cries of the crowd contradicted his conviction. When he could not convince the high priests and rulers of His innocence, he delivered the Savior to scourging first, in hopes that would satiate them, but to his disappointment, it was not enough, and the high priest and rulers demanded the crucifixion, which Pilate was compelled to execute.

Scourging and Mocking Him

Roman scourging was very brutal, much more severe than Jewish scourging. Jews only exposed the upper body part of the one to be scourged, while Romans exposed the whole body. For Jews, the whips had a limit—forty minus one—but the Romans observed no such limit, used extreme severity, and showed no compassion. Void of human emotions, they would whip criminals mercilessly and quite often criminals died under scourging. In fact, scourging was forbidden on Romans, and was designated for slaves and people from other nations under the Roman rule, whom they also classified as slaves (Acts 22:25).

After the Savior was scourged, they again removed His clothes and

إحداث المشاغبات والقلاقل و إهاجة المدينة بعمله الفتن وارتكابه القتل. من المحتمل أن باراباس كان من الحزب الذى يكره السلطان الرومانى.

مما يستحق الالتفات، أن باراباس كان مجرماً بذات الجرم الذى ادعى به رؤساء الكهنة كذباً على المخلص وهو الفتنة. لذلك لا يمكن تقديم برهان أكبر من هذا على انحطاط وخبث تلك الامة، وهو بذلهم كل ما فى استطاعتهم ليطلبوا من الحاكم الرومانى اطلاق سراح باراباس الاثيم وادانة المخلص البار. "حينئذ لما رأي بيلاطس انه لا فائدة من ذلك بل بالحرى يحدث شغب أخذ ماء وغسل يديه قدام الجمع قائلا: انى برئ من دم هذا البار أبصروا أنتم» (مت٢٧: ٢٤)، (تث٢١: ٦-٩)، لم يكن هذا القول مبرراً لبيلاطس، نعم وان كان قد غسل يديه بالماء ولكنه بذلك لم يغسل قلبه من الذنب، لانه سلم للموت من كان قد حكم ببراءته بمجرد سماعه صراخ الشعب بما هو مخالف لاعتقاده، فلما لم يقدر أن يُقنع الكهنة والرؤساء، أَسلمَ المخلص له المجد ليُجلد أولاً طلباً لإرضائهم، ولما أحبط عندما رأى إنهم لم يستكفوا بالجلد بل طلبوا أن يُصلب، حقق لهم بيلاطس إرادتهم بعد ذلك.

جلدوه واستهزأوا به:

وكان الجَلد عند الرومانيين فظيعاً جداً، بل كان أقسى كثيراً من جلد اليهود، لان اليهود كانوا يعرون فقط الجزء الأعلى من جسد المرغوب فى جلده، أما الرومانيون فكانوا يعرون الجسد كله. كانت عدد الجلدات عند اليهود محدوداً اى اربعين جلدة الا واحدة، واما عند الرومانيين فبلا عدد وبقسوة متناهية. فكانوا يجلدون المجرمين بلا رحمة ولا شفقة وكثيراً ما كان يموت البعض من المجرمين تحت الجلد. لذلك كان الجلد ممنوعاً على الرومانيين، بل خصوا به العبيد واهل البلاد التى تكون تحت سلطانهم، إذ كانوا عندهم بمنزلة عبيد (أع٢٢: ٢٥).

dressed Him in a scarlet robe; this is the attire of an army commander. The intention was to mock Jesus for proclaiming Himself a King. All their derision, however, was preordained by God to serve His divine purpose. What they used to mock Jesus, He used to establish Him as a King. The purple and scarlet robe is as a symbol that He is victorious; He was crowned with thorns because He is the King of heaven and earth; and a reed was placed in His hand because He clutches the scepter of sovereignty.

Vinegar Mixed with Bitter Herbs

After the soldiers ridiculed Jesus, they dressed Him in His own clothes and led Him outside the city to crucify Him at the place, called in Hebrew, Golgotha (the skull), which is a round high hill, void of rocks or trees and resembling the human skull. Some say it received this name because of the abundance of skulls of the slain thrown there. It was also said that Adam's skull was buried there.

When they arrived at this location, "they gave Him sour wine mingled with gall to drink. But when He had tasted it, He would not drink" (Mt 27:34). Most probably those who gave the Lord of glory this drink were Jews, as this was not a custom for the Romans. Jews offered this drink to whomever was condemned to death at their execution because the rabbis declared this to be godly and righteous, based on the Sage's advice: "Give strong drink to him who is perishing, and wine to those who are bitter of heart. Let him drink and forget his poverty, and remember his misery no more" (Prov 31:6–7). It seems that the Lord Christ tasted it out of courtesy to the one who offered this good deed, but refrained from drinking it, preferring to thoroughly feel His Passion, not wanting to distort His clarity of mind, and to sense all the pains of His crucifixion with full cognizance:

بعد ما جُلد المخلص له المجد نزعوا ثيابه والبسوه ثوباً قرمزياً، وهو ما كان يلبسه رؤساء الجيش، لكنهم البسوه إياه كاحتقار له لانهم زعموا أن مخلصنا له المجد إدَّعى بانه ملك، غير أن ما صنعوه به من استهزاء قد تعين من قبل الله ليدل على معانى إلهية، وتعييرهم له إستُخدم بالأكثر ليُثبت إنه ملك:

+ فانهم قد أُلبسوه القرمز والارجوان لأنه غالب.

+ قد كُلل بالشوك لأنه ملك السماء والارض.

+ قد وُضِعت فى يده قصبة لأنه قابض علي صولجان الملك.

الخل الممزوج بالمر:

وبعدما سَخَرَ الجند بيسوع البسوه ثيابه ومضوا به الى خارج المدينة ليصلب فى المكان الذى يسمى بالعبرانيه جلجثة ومعناه الجمجمة، وهو عبارة عن اكمة مرتفعة مستديرة خالية من الصخور والاشجار تشبه جمجمة الانسان. وقال بعضهم سُميت بهذا الاسم لكثرة ما طرح فيها من جماجم القتلى. وقيل أيضاً أن جمجمة آدم كانت مدفونه هناك.

فلما وصلوا به الي ذلك المكان أعطوه خلاً ممزوجاً بمرارة ليشرب ولما ذاق لم يرد أن يشرب (مت ٢٧: ٣٤)، ومن المرجح أن الذين قدموا للسيد المسيح له المجد هذا الشراب هم من اليهود، لانه لم يكن ذلك من عوائد الرومان. ولان اليهود كانوا يتبرعون به لكل محكوم عليه بالموت عند قتله. ولان الربانيين أعلنوا أنه من أعمال التقوى والبر بُناءً على قول الحكيم "اعطوا مسكراً لهالك وخمراً لمرى النفس. يشرب وينسي فقره ولا يذكر تعبه بعد (أم ٣١: ٦، ٧)،" ويظهر إن السيد المسيح له المجد ذاقه إكراماً لمن أسدى له هذا المعروف بإعطائه إياه ولكنه أبي أن يشربه لأنه فضل أن يكون له الحس التام بالآمه، ولم يشأ أن يُعكر صفاء عقله، ليكابد جميع آلام

"Shall I not drink the cup which My Father has given Me?" (Jn 18:11). As for the drink, it was of bitter herbs like wormwood mingled with poppy seed juice and acidic wine (differing slightly from vinegar). The intention in blending it with the wine was to provide a potent effect, so that by simply drinking from it, the crucified becomes oblivious to being dead or alive.

Pain of the Cross

"There They Crucified Him" (Lk 23:33). Roman crucifixion is the most agonizing and severest form of torture endured by a transgressor. In addition to the crucifixion and scourging, our Lord endured consistent mockery and derision throughout this horrible ordeal. There was great pain arising from the duration the crucified remained alive (three days or longer), being drenched in sweat, hungry, and feverish (from inflamed wounds). The crucified was placed in such a position that the slightest movement caused extreme sharp pain to penetrate throughout his whole body from the strain of the nails in his hands and feet. Likewise, the blood accumulating in the lungs and pressing on the heart caused indescribable and excruciating pain accompanied by great thirst. Crucifixion was humiliating to the extent that Romans would never execute such a ruling against a Roman; it was reserved for slaves, thieves, the insubordinate, and criminals.

Crucifixion as a Form of Punishment

Those condemned to crucifixion were first scourged, and then, each carried his cross to the crucifixion site, a specific location outside the city where many people gathered to deride and mock them as an example of deterrence for others. When they reached the crucifixion site, they would strip them and offer them an intoxicant (as described earlier). For Jews, crucifixion was not a form of punishment. It was forbidden for a Jew to crucify a Jew. As for the comment in the Torah about hanging on the wood ["He who is hanged is accursed of God" (Deut 21:23)], it is what is generally known

الصلب وهو فى حالة الصحو. لأنه الكأس الذى أعطاه الآب ليشربه (يو١٨: ١١)، أما الشراب فكان من الأعشاب المرة كالافسنتين وأمثاله، ممزوج بنقيع بزر الخشخاش وخل حامض يختلف عن الخل قليلاً، وغايتهم من مزج الخمر به ليكون شديد التأثير، حتى إنه بمجرد ما يأخذ منه المصلوب لا يدرى ولا يشعر أن كان ميتاً أو حياً.

آلآم الصليب:

"حينئذ صلبوا يسوع" (لو ٢٣: ٣٣)، كان الصلب عند الرومانيين من أشد العذابات المبرحة وأوفر القصاصات الآماً للمذنبين لما فيه من التشهير والعار الذى يلحق بالشخص المصلوب، والالآم الشديدة التى تنتج عن طول المدة، فقد يبقى المصلوب معلقاً حياً ثلاثة أيام أو أكثر، فيعتريه جوع وأرق وحمى من إلتهاب الجراح، لأن المصلوب كان يوضع على هيئة بحيث أن أدنى حركة يأتيها تسبب له ألماً شديداً جداً فى كل أجزاء الجسم من شدة المسامير فى اليدين والرجلين. و كذلك الدم الذى يتجمع فى الرئتين ويضغط على القلب كان يسبب ألماً شديداً فوق التصور لا يُطاق ولا يُحتمل مصحوباً بعطش شديد. وكان الصلب مهيناً حتى أن الرومان لم يقاصوا به البتة رعاياهم من الرومانيين، بل كانوا يعاقبون به فقط الأرقاء واللصوص والعصاة والمجرمين.

عقوبة الصلب:

كان المحكوم عليهم بالصلب يُجلدون أولا ثم يَحملون الصليب الى محل الصلب الذى كان يُعين فى مكان مشهور خارج المدينة حيث يجتمع كثيرون من الناس، وذلك لأجل إحتقارهم والإستهزاء بهم ليصبحوا عبرة لغيرهم. وكان متى وصلوا الى محل الصلب يعروهم ثم كانوا يقدمون لهم شرابا مُخدِراً كما مر. والصلب لم يكن من أنواع العقوبات عند اليهود، وكان من المحال أن يَصلِب يهودي يهودياً، أما ما ورد فى التوراة عن التعليق على خشبة فالمقصود به ما يُعرف عند الجميع بالشنق[٣٥]

today as hanging. Crucifixion originated in Persia, where it was used as a punishment for Egyptians, Greeks, and Romans. Alexander the Great, in conquering the city of Tyre, crucified 2,000 of its residents. Romans did not decree upon Romans death by crucifixion, but reserved it for slaves, persons committing the vilest crimes, and the inhabitants of countries they conquered (whom they classified as slaves). The Roman ruler, Crispus, decorated the path from the city of Kibeu to the city of Rome with the crosses of those who offended the Roman Empire. Caesar Augustus crucified 6,000 slaves on the Island of Sicily because they disobeyed him.

Method of Crucifixion

The crucifix was composed of two perpendicular pieces of wood, with a rod placed at the foot, to bear part of his weight and hold him upright, lest the spot where the nails were inserted tear the skin of the crucified and they fall off the cross. One method was to erect the cross, and lift up the crucified and nail him while in the air. Most often, after removing the crucified's clothes, they would place the cross horizontally on the ground, and stretch him out on it and nail his hands and feet to the wood of the cross. Often times, they would only nail the hands, and tie the legs to the cross with ropes. They would position the cross vertically, and elevate the person being crucified, crucifying him while suspended above ground. As for our Lord of glory's crucifixion, it was by nailing the hands and feet (as confirmed in the Gospel according to St. Luke (Lk 24:39–40)). Then they would lift up the cross with the crucified, and erect it vertically into the hole prepared for this sole purpose. Sometimes, they would thrust the cross into the hole with great speed and violently, that it would magnify the crucified's pain and suffering. The crucified was about one handbreadth above the ground. When the soldiers nailed our Savior to the cross, He prayed saying, "Father, forgive them, for they do not know what they do" (Lk 23:34).

(تث ٢١: ٢٣). أصل الصلب كان فى بلاد الفرس وعاقب به كل من المصريين واليونانيين والرومانيين. فالإسكندر الكبير عند إفتتاحه لمدينة صور صَلب من أهلها الفين. والرومانيون لم يوقعوا علي رومانى حُكم الموت بالصلب، بل خصوا به العبيد ومن يرتكب أشر الآثام وأهل الولايات التى إستولوا عليها لانهم يحسبونهم كالعبيد. وكراسبوس القائد الرومانى سيج الطريق من مدينة كبيو إلى مدينة روميه بصلبان العبيد الذين عصوا الدولة الرمانية. وصَلَبَ أغسطس قيصر ستة آلاف عبد فى جزيرة صقلية أي سيسيليا لأنهم عصوه.

كيفية الصلب:

وكان الصليب يُركّب من قطعتين متعارضتين من الخشب فى إحداهما عمود يدخل بين رجلى المصلوب ليحمل بعض ثقله لئلا يتمزق محل مدخل المسامير فيسقط المصلوب. وكانوا ينصبون الصليب رأسياً ويرفعون الشخص المراد صلبه ويسمرونه وهو مرتفع عن الأرض. وغالباً ما كانوا يضعون الصليب أفقياً على الأرض ويمدون المراد صلبه عليه بعدما يعرونه من ثيابه، ثم يسمرون يديه ورجليه بالمسامير على خشبة الصليب. ثم يرفعون الصليب بالمصلوب بعيداً عن الأرض بمقدار زراع واحد، ثم ينصبونه رأسياً فى حفرة يعدونها لذلك، وأحياناً كانوا ينزلون بالصليب فى الحفرة بسرعة وعنف شديدين ليضاعفوا عذاب المصلوب. وقد سيدنا له المجد فصُلب بتسمير يديه ورجليه بدليل ماجاء فى بشارة معلمنا لوقا (لو٢٤: ٣٩، ٤٠)، فلما سمر العسكر مخلصنا له المجد على الصليب صلى قائلاً «يا أبتاه إغفر لهم لأنهم لا يعلمون ماذا يفعلون»(لو٢٣: ٣٤).

Title of the Crucified

It was custom for the condemned to bear the inscription of his accusation, so when he reached the crucifixion site, it was placed above his head. For Pilate, the accusation against the Lord Christ was: "THIS IS JESUS THE KING OF THE JEWS" (Mt 27:37). Thus, the insignia was written in the three popular languages in Syria at that time: Hebrew, Greek, and Latin. By inscribing this sign, Pilate intended to ridicule and mock the Jews by crucifying their king. The chief priests objected to the inscription, but he did not care for, or pay attention to their protests and said, "What I have written, I have written" (Jn 19:22). Therefore, the title that the wise men gave Christ at His birth glorifying Him, Pilate also gave to Him at His death.

Darkness over the Whole Earth

Jesus was hung on the cross before noon, and from the sixth hour to the ninth hour, there was darkness over the whole earth (Mt 27:34; Mk 15:33; Lk 23:44). This darkness was a miracle because the sun could not eclipse except when the moon is a crescent; it was the 15th of the month and a full moon. This was a total eclipse, not a partial! Nature dressed in mourning over what humanity did to the Creator of Existence, the Coordinator of Creation, the Light of the World, and the Sun of Righteousness.

He Was Wounded for Our Transgressions

Listen, O my beloved, while I mention the shocking pains which our Savior suffered from the Jews. They arrested Him in an inhuman way, treated Him with barbaric cruelty, and bound Him and took Him like a criminal to the council of Caiaphas and Annas, while slapping, beating, and spitting on His honorable face. They branded Him with their unjust judgment and handed Him to Pilate. Pilate, then, dressed Him in white (in the appearance of a lunatic) and sent Him to Herod, who after examining Him and finding no

عنوان المصلوب:

وكانت العادة أن يحمل المحكوم عليه بالصلب إعلان العلة التى صُلب لأجلها حتى إذا وصلوا محل الصلب تُوضَع فوق رأسه. فكانت علة السيد المسيح عند بيلاطس (هذا هو يسوع ملك اليهود) (مت ٢٧: ٣٧)، وكَتب هذا العنوان بثلاث لغات كانت شائعة فى سوريا وقتئذ، وهى العبرانية واليونانية واللاتينية. وقصد بيلاطس بذلك العنوان تعيير اليهود بصلب ملكهم والتشهير بهم. فاعترض الرؤساء علي ما كُتب لكن بيلاطس لم يُبال بهم ولم يذعن لقولهم بل قال «ما كتبت قد كتبت» (يو ١٩: ٢٢)، فما لقَّب المجوس به السيد المسيح عند ميلاده تمجيداً له، لقَّبه به أيضاً بيلاطس عند موته.

الظلمة على الأرض:

علق مخلصنا له المجد على الصليب قبل الظهر. «ولما كانت الساعة السادسة، كانت ظلمة على الأرض كلها الى الساعة التاسعة» (مت٢٧: ٣٤)، (مر١٥: ٣٣)، (لو٢٣: ٤٤)، فكانت هذه الظلمة معجزة لأنه لا يمكن أن يحصل كسوف للشمس إلا والقمر هلال. وكان يومئذ اليوم الخامس عشر من الشهر. وكان القمر بدراً وكان هذا الكسوف كلياً وليس جزئياً، فقد لبست الطبيعة أثواب الحداد إظهاراً لما فعله البشر بخالق الكون، مدبر الخليقة، نور العالم، وشمس البر.

مجروح لأجل معاصينا (أش ٥٣: ٥):

إسمعوا أيها الأحباء ذكر ما قاساه مخلصنا له المجد من الآلآمات المبرحة من اليهود، فإنهم قبضوا عليه بشكل لا يتفق مع الإنسانية، وعاملوه بقسوة بربرية، فأخذوه موثقاً الى مجلس قيافا وحنان بين لَطْم وضَرْب وبَصْق على الوجه الكريم، وإستهزاء به كمجرم وهو البار القدوس. هناك أصدروا عليه حكمهم الظالم، وسلموه الى بيلاطس، وبيلاطس ألبسه لباساً أبيض كمجنون وأرسله الى هيرودس، ولما فحصه

reason deserving of death, sent Him back to Pilate, who was compelled to condemn Him to death after scourging. The Jews bribed the scourgers to kill Him under the whips, so they whipped Him with all their brutality, so much so, that they tore apart His pure body. In staying on course with their viciousness, they placed on His holy head, instead of a diadem, a crown of thorns sharper than nails, which penetrated His forehead; and instead of a royal robe, they placed on His shoulders a red robe; and instead of the scepter of rule, they handed Him a reed.

His body grew feverish due to the wound from carrying the heavy massive cross, trudging through the crowded streets of Jerusalem. On His journey were the mocking of the crowds, the derision of rivals, the attacks of the vulgar, the insults of bandits, and the vengeance of the enemies. He agonized under it at the throes of death, and sometimes fell upon the stones, and rose again—pale faced, drained of strength, and drenched in blood until He reached the Golgotha altar. There, He was laid on the cross to be pierced by the nails penetrating His body to the cross. Thus, Isaiah's prophecy was fulfilled: "He has no form or comeliness; and when we see Him, there is no beauty that we should desire Him. He is despised and rejected by men, a Man of sorrows and acquainted with grief. And we hid, as it were, our faces from Him; He was despised, and we did not esteem Him. Surely He has borne our griefs and carried our sorrows; yet we esteemed Him stricken, smitten by God, and afflicted. But He was wounded for our transgressions, He was bruised for our iniquities" (Is 53:2-5). Nature was affected by this scene: the sun untimely hid its rays—ashamed to see its Creator hanging naked on the Cross; creation stared at Him as did shameless Ham (Gen 9:22–23); the earth shook in shock and the rocks split in horror over the Lord of glory, as if saying, "Let me swallow the wicked ones who do not know their Creator, by whom they live, move, and have their being" (Acts 17:28), as it swallowed Korah, Dathan, and Abiram (Num 16:31–32).

This all happened to our Savior for our sake. Are we fulfilling our duty toward our Creator? The Jews' crucifixion is not less harsh than ours: some of us add to the weight of His crucifixion, others ridicule Him more than

هـيرودس ولم يجـد فيـه علـة يسـتوجب عليهـا المـوت، أعـاده ثانيـة الى بيلاطـس فحكـم عليـه بالمـوت بعـد الجلـد. ورشـا اليهـود الجلاديـن لـكى يميتـوه تحـت السـياط، فجلـدوه بـكل قسـوة حتـى مزقـوا جسـده الطاهـر تمزيقـاً، وأتمـوا عملهـم البربـرى بوضعهـم عـلى هامتـه المقدسـة إكليـلاً مـن الشـوك أحـد مـن المسـامير عوضـاً عـن التـاج فخـدش جبينـه الطلـق، وبـدلاً مـن البرفـير وضعـوا عـلى كتفـه ثوبـاً أحمـر، وعوضـاً عـن صولجـان الملـك أمسـكوه قصبـة.

وقـد أتخـن جسـده بالجـراح مـن جـراء حمـل الصليـب الضخـم الثقيـل سـائراً بـه فى شـوارع أورشـليم، بـين سـخرية الجمـع، وإهانـة الخصـوم، وتهكـم السـفلة، وشـتائم الاجـلاف، وتشـفى الاعـداء، يـئن تحتـه أنـين المحتـضر، فيقـع تـارة عـلي الحجـارة وينهـض أخـرى، خائـر القـوى، شـاحب الوجـه، دامـى الاعضـاء، حتـى بلـغ مذبـح الجلجلـة، وهنـاك جـرى مقتلـه بحـراب المسـامير عـلى الصليـب، [فكملـت نبـوة أشـعياء قائـلاً «لا صـورة لـه ولا جـمال فننظـر اليـه ولا منظـر فنشـتهيه، محتقـر ومخـذول مـن النـاس، رجـل أوجـاع ومختـبر الحـزن، وكمسَّـتر عنـه وجوهنـا، محتقـر فلـم نعتـد بـه، لكـن أحزاننـا حملهـا، وأوجاعنـا تحملهـا، ونحـن حسـبناه مصابـاً مضروبـاً مـن النـاس ومذلـولاً. وهـو مجـروح لأجـل معاصينـا، مسـحوق لأجـل أثامنـا(أش٥٣: ٢-٥)] فتأثـرت الطبيعـة مـن هـول هـذا المنظـر، الشـمس حجبـت نورهـا بغـير أوان خجـلاً مـن أن تـرى مبدعهـا معلقـاً عـلى الصليـب عاريـاً والخليقـة تتفـرس فيـه مثـل حـام الوقـح (تـك ٩: ٢٢-٢٣). والأرض تزلزلـت إضطرابـاً والصخـور تشـققت إلتياعـاً عـلى رب المجـد،. ولسـان حالهـا يقـول دعنـى أبتلـع الأشرار الذيـن لم يعرفـوا خالقهـم الـذى بـه يحيـون ويتحركـون ويوجـدون (أع ١٧: ٢٨)، كـما إبتلعـت قـورح وداثـان وأبـيرام (عـدد١٦: ٣١، ٣٢).

هـذا ماحـل بالمخلـص لـه المجـد لأجلنـا، فهـل نحـن قائمـون بمـا يجـب علينـا نحـو خالقنـا؟ فـما صَلْـب اليهـود لـه بأكـثر قسـوة منـا، فمنـا مـن أزاد صليبـه ثقـلاً، ومنـا مـن هـزأ بـه أكـثر مـن هـيرودس، ومنـا مـن باعـه بأشـد خيانـة مـن يهـوذا، ومنـا مـن جلـده بقسـاوة افظـع مـن قسـاوة العسـكر والجنـد، ومنـا مـن غـرز فى هامتـه أشـواكاً أحَـد مـن

Herod, while others may sell Him with a more piercing betrayal than Judas. Some may whip Him as intensely as the soldiers, some may act like the sharp thorns on His crown placed upon His forehead, still others increase the number of His nails, while others pierce Him, but not with a spear as did His murderers, but with the spears of our sins.

The One who stirred the thief on His right hand[37] to repentance can alone enlighten our hearts to see the repugnance of sin, and return to Him—our beloved Creator, with a repented heart.

His Cry on the Cross

At the ninth hour, Jesus cried out with a loud voice, "Eli, Eli, lama sabachthani," a Hebrew phrase bearing the meaning, "My God, My God, why have You forsaken Me?" (Mt 27:46; Ps 22:1; cf. Heb 5:7). (It appeared in the Gospel according to St. Mark as, "Eloi, Eloi" (Mk 15:34), a similar expression, except that our teacher, St. Mark, transcribed it in the Syrian language, as the Lord Christ pronounced it). This bitter depression and great anguish pushed our Savior to this horrific outcry: "My God, My God, why have You forsaken Me?" because He felt the extent of the pain that He bore for the sake of our sins while on the Cross. He stood instead of us before Divine Justice to pay our dues. He tasted death for every person (Heb 2:9), and became sin for us, He, who knows no sin, that we might become the righteousness of God in Him (Cf. 2 Cor 5:21). This fulfills what Isaiah said: "Yet it pleased the Lord to bruise Him; He has put Him to grief. When You make His soul an offering for sin... But He was wounded for our transgressions, He was bruised for our iniquities; the chastisement for our peace was upon Him, and by His stripes we are healed" (Is 53:10,5), St. Peter also said: "[Christ] suffered once for sins, the just for the unjust, that He might bring us to God" (1 Pet 3:18).

After this, Jesus, knowing that all things were now accomplished, that the Scripture might be fulfilled, said, "I thirst!" Now a vessel full of sour wine was sitting there; and they filled a sponge with sour wine, put it

أكليل صالبيه، ومنا من زاد مسامير صلبه عدداً، ومنا من طعنه لا بحربة كقاتليه بل بحراب الخطايا والذنوب

«اللهم يامن ألهم اللص اليمين[٣٧] التوبة، وهداه الى سبل الرشاد، أنت وحدك القادر أن تنير عيون قلوبنا فنرى شناعة الخطية ونرجع الى خالقنا نادمين على ما إرتكبناه من المعاصي والشرور».

الصراخ على الصليب:

وفي وقت الساعة التاسعة صرخ يسوع بصوت عظيم قائلاً "إيلى إيلى لما شبقتني" لفظة عبرانية مكررة معناها «إلهى إلهى لماذا تركتنى» (مت ٢٧: ٤٦)، (مز٢٢: ١)، (عب٥: ٧) وجاء فى انجيل معلمنا مرقس "ألوى ألوى" (مر١٥: ٣٤) وهذا اللفظ أيضاً مثل «إيلى إيلى» إلا أن معلمنا مرقس نقلها بلفظه السريانى كما نطق به السيد المسيح له المجد، إن هذه الكآبة المرة والضيقة الشديدة التى إضطرت مخلصنا له المجد إلى هذا الصراخ المخيف "إلهى إلهى لماذا تركتني" هو إنه شعر بشدة الآلآم التى تحملها لأجل خطايانا وهو على الصليب وشناعة الخطية التى إرتكبها الانسان، وقيامه نيابة عنا أمام العدل الالهى ليفيه حقه إذ ذاق الموت عن كل إنسان (عب ٢: ٩)، «لأنه جعل الذى لم يعرف خطية، خطية لأجلنا لنصير نحن بر الله فيه» (٢كو٥: ٢١)، وهذا إتمام لقول أشعياء «أما الرب فسُر بأن يسحقه بالحزن. إن جعل نفسه ذبيحة أثم» (أش ٥٣: ١٠)، «وهو مجروح لأجل معاصينا مسحوق لأجل آثامنا تأديب سلامنا عليه وبحبره شفينا» (أش ٥٣: ٥)، وكما قال بطرس أيضاً «فإن المسيح أيضاً تألم مرة واحدة من أجل الخطايا، البار من أجل الاثمة، لكي يقربنا إلى الله» (١بط ٣: ١٨).

«بَعْدَ هَذَا رَأَى يَسُوعُ أَنَّ كُلَّ شَيْءٍ قَدْ كَمَلَ فَلِكَيْ يَتِمَّ الْكِتَابُ قَالَ: «أَنَا عَطْشَانُ» وَكَانَ إِنَاءٌ مَوْضُوعاً مَمْلُوّاً خَلاًّ فَمَلأُوا إِسْفِنْجَةً مِنَ الْخَلِّ وَوَضَعُوهَا عَلَى زُوفَا وَقَدَّمُوهَا إِلَى فَمِهِ، فَلَمَّا أَخَذَ يَسُوعُ الْخَلَّ قَالَ: «قَدْ أُكْمِلَ». وَنَكَّسَ رَأْسَهُ وَأَسْلَمَ الرُّوحَ» (يو١٩:

on hyssop, and put it to His mouth. So when Jesus had received the sour wine, He said, "It is finished!" And bowing His head, He gave up His spirit (Jn 19:28-30). After this, Jesus cried out again with a loud voice and gave up the spirit (Mt 27:50; Mk 15:37; Lk 23:46); perhaps, this cry was the shout of joy because He had fulfilled our redemption.

Crying with a loud voice at His death proves that He did not die out of weakness or fatigue, but was in full strength.

His Seven Words and His Death

He uttered seven words while on the cross—three before the darkness and four after:

1) Forgiving His crucifiers: "Father, forgive them, for they do not know what they do" (Lk 23:34).

2) Promising the thief [on His right] salvation: "Assuredly, I say to you, today you will be with Me in Paradise" (Lk 23:43).

3) Entrusting His mother to the beloved disciple, John: "Woman, behold your son... Behold your mother!" (Jn 19:26–27).

4) Crying to God: "My God, My God, why have You forsaken Me?" (Mt 27:46).

5) "I thirst" (Jn 19:28).

6) "It is finished" (Jn 19:30).

7) Giving up His pure spirit to the Father: "Father, into Your hands I commit My spirit" (Lk 23:46).

٢٨-٣٠). وبعد ذلك صرخ يسوع أيضاً بصوت عظيم وأسلم الروح» (مت٢٧: ٥٠)، (مر١٥: ٣٧)، (لو٢٣: ٤٦)، ولعل هذا الصراخ كان هتاف الفرح لأنه أكمل عمل الفداء.

أما صراخه بصوت عظيم على الصليب فهذا دليل على أنه لم يمت بضعف وعياء بل إنه كان فى تمام قوته.

كلماته السبع وموته:

وقد نطق مخلصنا له المجد بسبع كلمات وهو على الصليب، ثلاثة قبل الظلمة، وأربعة بعدها وهم:

١- «يا أبتاه إغفر لهم لأنهم لا يعلمون ماذا يفعلون» (لو٢٣: ٣٤) إشارة الى غفرانه لصالبيه.

٢- «الحق أقول لك إنك اليوم تكون معى فى الفردوس» (لو٢٣: ٤٣) إشارة الى وعده للص بالخلاص.

٣- «يا إمرأة هوذا إبنك» ثم «هوذا أمك» (يو١٩: ٢٦، ٢٧) إشارة الى تسليم أمه ليوحنا تلميذه ليرعاها.

٤- صراخه قائلاً «إيلى إيلى لما شبقتنى أى إلهى إلهى لماذا تركتنى» (مت٢٧: ٤٦).

٥- «أنا عطشان» (يو١٩: ٢٨).

٦- «قد أكمل» (يو١٩: ٣٠).

٧- أودع روحه النقية للآب «يا أبتاه فى يديك أستودع روحى» (لو٢٣: ٤٦).

His Divinity Parted Not from His Humanity

We know that at His Incarnation, the Lord Christ was perfect God incarnate: as His Divinity united with His humanity without mixing, mingling, or changing. Therefore, according to His Humanity, He was susceptible to all of life's difficulties: hunger and thirst (Jn 4:7), weariness (Jn 4:6), crying (Heb 5:7), tears (Jn 11:35), sorrow (Mk 14:34), and all the other effects of the world—except sin (Heb 4:15). Yet, according to His Divinity, He vastly surpassed this: He satiated the hungry (Jn 6:10), quenched the thirsty (Jn 7:37; Mt 26:27; Jn 4:15; Rev 21:6), relieved the exhausted (Mt 11:28), consoled the sorrowful (Jn 11:40–44; 2 Cor 1:3–4), and saved the weak from temptation (Mt 14:28–31; 1 Cor 10:13).

The Holy Spirit testified to this through the writings of the holy apostles. St. Peter said, "Who Himself bore our sins in His own body on the tree" (1 Pet 2:24). St. Paul said, "God did by sending His own Son in the likeness of sinful flesh, on account of sin: He condemned sin in the flesh" (Rom 8:3). Again, St. Peter declares, "Put to death in the flesh but made alive by the Spirit" (1 Pet 3:18), because it was written of Him: "Who alone has immortality, dwelling in unapproachable light" (1 Tim 6:16).

At His death, He gave up His pure spirit, saying to His Father, "Father, into Your hands I commit My spirit." Thus, He died according to His Humanity, while His Divinity did not part from His body for a single moment nor a twinkle of an eye, not before crucifixion, during, nor after crucifixion. In declaring this, we say that it is impossible for the Lord Christ to be two persons—one contradicting the other: one born and the other not. One cannot amaze with wonders, while the other receives mockery; neither can one be crucified while the other not crucified. The one born, the wonderworker, and the crucified are all one. This is the apostolic faith, the concurrence of the evangelists, and the fathers' aphorisms.

That He is the Immortal and Living is evinced from a profound sign when the soldier pierced Jesus's side, and out flowed water and blood from His side. Church history, taken from early tradition, mentions that when Joseph and Nicodemus came to embalm the Master, Joseph held His hand

اللآهوت لم يفارق الناسوت:

بما إننا قد عرفنا أن السيد المسيح له المجد عند تجسده كان إلهاً كاملا متأنساً، وقد إتحد لاهوته بناسوته بدون إختلاط ولا إمتزاج ولاتغيير، فكان بناسوته قابلاً لكل ما يطرأ عليه من صعوبات الحياة، كالجوع والعطش (يو٤: ٧) والتعب (يو٤: ٦) والصراخ (عب٥: ٧) والبكاء (يو١١: ٣٥) والحزن (مر١٤: ٣٤) وسائر التجارب العالمية ماعدا الخطية (عب٤: ١٥)، وأما بلاهوته فمتعال عن ذلك علواً كبيراً فيهب الشبع للجوعان (يو٦: ١٠) ويروى العطشان (مت٢٦: ٢٧)، (يو٤: ١٥)، (يو٧: ٣٧)، (رؤ٢١: ٦)، ويريح من التعب (مت١١: ٢٨) ويعزى الحزين (يو١١: ٤٠)، (٢كو١: ٣-٤) ويخلص من التجارب (مت١٤: ٢٨-٣١)، (١كو١٠: ١٣).

وقد شهد الروح القدس بذلك علي أفواه الرسل القديسين، فيقول بطرس الرسول «الذى حمل هو خطايانا فى جسده على الخشبة» (١بط ٢: ٢٤)، وقال الرسول «إذ أرسل الله ابنه فى شبه جسد الخطية ولاجل الخطية دان الخطية في الجسد» (رو٨: ٣)، وبصريح العبارة يبرهن بطرس عن موته بالجسد قائلاً «مماتاً فى الجسد ولكن محيياً في الروح (١بط٣: ١٨)، لأنه مكتوب عنه «الذى وحده له عدم الموت ساكناً فى نور لايدنى منه» (١تي٦: ١٦).

فعند موته أسلم روحه الطاهرة قائلا لأبيه: «يا أبتاه في يديك أستودع روحى» وهكذا مات بناسوته ومع ذلك لاهوته لم يفارق ناسوته أى جسده لحظة واحدة ولا طرفة عين لا قبل الصلب ولا حين الصلب ولا بعد الصلب. وإذ تقرر ذلك نقول أنه لايمكن أن يكون فى المسيح فِعلان، أحدهما يضاد الآخر، واحد يولد والآخر لا يولد، واحد يبهر بالعجائب والآخر تقع عليه الاهانات، واحد يُصلب والآخر لا يُصلب. بل أن المولود، والصانع العجائب، والمصلوب، هو واحد. هذا هو الايمان الرسولي وإتفاق أصوات البشيرين وأقوال الآباء.

ومما يبرهن على أنه الحى غير المائت، إنه لما طعنه أحد الجنود بالحربة خرج من جنبه ماء علامة على أنه حى ولن يموت. وجاء فى تاريخ الكنيسة الذى أُخِذَ عن

and said, "Would this awesome hand that created all die, and could I now embalm it!" Christ opened His eyes and smiled, at which Joseph cried out, "Holy God, Holy Mighty, Holy Immortal." Hence, the Church arranged this chant among her hymns for Passion Week.

Therefore, it is a fact that our Lord's acceptance of the passion and death was not with regards to His Divinity. His Divinity is impassible; therefore, the impact did not reach the Divinity, being united with His Humanity (a full personal natural hypostatic union): indivisible, inseparable, and irreproducible.

The Reason for His Death and None Other

They Have All Turned Aside

Before beings were created, and even before the creation of time, God knew by His foreknowledge that man would sin and do evil. Since "the wages of sin is death" (Rom 6:23), God, out of His abundant mercy did not wish the death of man whom He was about to create, so He planned his salvation before Adam appeared on the face of the earth. Salvation could not occur except through the mediation of an unblemished, righteous, Holy One, on whose mouth there is no deceit, who is outside the human race, and without sin. An angel, archangel, prophet, or saint could not fulfill this. The angelic nature differs from the human nature, and the prophets and saints were born with the original sin, which affects the whole human race—no one being is exempted. According to St. Paul, "Therefore, just as through one man sin entered the world, and death through sin, and thus death spread to all men, because all sinned" (Rom 5:12). Also, "'There is none righteous, no, not one; there is none who understands; there is none who seeks after God. They have all turned aside; they have together become unprofitable; there is none who does good, no, not one'" (Rom 3:10–12).

التقليد القديم أن يوسف ونقوديموس لما شرعا فى تحنيط السيد المسيح أمسك يوسف يده وقال هذه اليد العظيمة التى خلقت المخلوقات تموت وأنا أحنطها؟ ففتح السيد المسيح عينيه وتبسم فى وجهه، فصرخ عند ذلك يوسف قائلا «قدوس الله، قدوس القوى، قدوس الحي الذى لا يموت». ولذلك قد رتبت الكنيسة هذه التسبحة بين ترنيماتها أيضاً فى إسبوع الالام.

إذن فليكن معلوماً أن قبول ربنا الآلام والموت لم يكن من حيثية لاهوته الأقدس، إذ أن اللاهوت منزه عن كافة الانفعالات، لذلك لم تتطرق إليه التأثيرات بما أنه متحد بالناسوت إتحاداً ذاتياً طبيعياً أقنومياً لا يقبل الانفصال ولا الافتراق ولا يشوبه تثنية.

السبب الذى مات لأجله يسوع دون سواه

الجميع زاغوا (رو٣: ١٢):

قبل أن تُخلق الكائنات، وقبل أن تتعين الازمان، عَلِمَ الله بسابق عِلمه أن الانسان سيخطئ ويعمل الشر على الارض، وبما أن «أجرة الخطية هى موت» (رو٦: ٢٣)، وكان الله من فرط رحمته لا يشاء أن يهلك الانسان الذى هو مزمع أن يخلقه. فدبر الله أمر خلاصه قبل أن يظهر فى عالم الوجود. ولما كان ذلك الخلاص لا يتم الا بواسطة بار قدوس لا عيب فيه، ولا يوجد في فمه غش، خارج عن الجنس البشرى، منزه عن الخطية، وبما أن هذا الامر لا يقدر أن يقوم به ملاك أو رئيس ملائكة أو نبي أو قديس، لان طبيعة الملائكة غير طبيعة البشر. وبما أن الانبياء و القديسون مولدون بالخطية الجدية التى عمت جميع النوع الانساني، ولم يستثن منها أحد كقول بولس الرسول «من أجل ذلك كأنما بانسان واحد دخلت الخطية إلى العالم وبالخطية الموت وهكذا إجتاز الموت إلى جميع الناس إذ أخطأ الجميع» (رو٥: ١٢)، كما هو مكتوب أنه «ليس بار ولا واحد، ليس من يفهم، ليس من يطلب الله، الجميع زاغوا وفسدوا معاً، ليس من يعمل صلاحاً ليس ولا واحد» (رو٣: ١٠-١٢).

Salvation Through the Son

A transgressor cannot save a fellow transgressor, nor can a needy person satisfy the wants of a fellow destitute. The Almighty God saw that this redemption could not be fulfilled except through the second hypostasis, through whom the creation was formed, as our teacher St. John the Evangelist testified: "All things were made through Him, and without Him nothing was made that was made" (Jn 1:3). Therefore, it was the responsibility of the One who created all things to be the Savior, and none other. "God sent forth His Son, born of a woman, born under the law, to redeem those who were under the law, that we might receive the adoption as sons" (Gal 4:4–5). Thus, He took the form of a servant, which was defiled by sin, to renew it once more and restore it to its original glory. All three hypostases participated in humanity's salvation: the Father's justice was fulfilled; the Son paid the debt for mankind; and the Holy Spirit remitted the sins.

Justice and Mercy

This is the reason God took the form of a bondservant—to judge sin in the flesh. God was able to save man by a word, as He created him by a word, but because He is just, He saw that there was no forgiveness except by the shedding of blood. Therefore, there was a necessity for this amazing incarnation, one beyond nature, to fulfill Divine Justice: "The soul who sins shall die" (Ezra 18:20). God's mercy had to fulfill the work of redemption for sinful man. In this way, God is simultaneously just and merciful. Justice received its due by the death of the Son on the wood of the cross, and mercy interceded in fulfilling salvation. Thus, God's justice and mercy were at equilibrium as each one was affirmed in accordance.

الخلاص بالإبن:

بما إنـه لا يقـدر المذنـب أن يخلـص مذنبـاً مثلـه، كـما وأن المحتـاج لا يسـد عـوز مـن يشـبهه فى الاحتيـاج، رأى اللـه -لـه المجـد- أن لايتـم هـذا الفـداء إلا بالاقنـوم الثـانى الـذى بواسـطته قـد صـورت الخليقـة كـما شـهد بذلـك معلمنـا يوحنـا الانجيـلى «كل شئ بـه كان وبغـيره لم يكـن شـئ مـما كان»(يـو١: ٣)، فوجـب بمـن أوجـد الموجـودات أن يكـون بـه الخـلاص دون سـواه فأرسـل اللـه إبنـه، مولـوداً مـن إمـرأة، مولـوداً تحـت النامـوس ليفتـدي الذيـن تحـت النامـوس لننـال التبنـى (غـل٤: ٤-٥)، فلبـس صـورة الانسـان التـى كانـت قـد أفسـدتها الخطيـة ليجددهـا مـرة ثانيـة ويعيـد لهـا مجدهـا الاول، وكان ذلـك باجـماع الثلاثـة الاقانيـم عـلى خـلاص الانسـان. فـالآب إسـتوفى عدلـه، الابـن قـد قـدم عنـه الوفـاء، والـروح القـدس غفـر الخطايـا.

العدل والرحمة:

فهـذا السـبب الـذى جعـل اللـه أن يتخـذ صـورة عبـد وجسـد انسـان خاطـئ ليديـن الخطيـة في الجسـد وكان اللـه قـادراً أن يخلـص الانسـان بكلمـة كـما خلـق العـالم بكلمـة ولكـن بمـا انـه عـادل رأى أن لا تحصـل مغفـرة إلا بسـفك دم، فلـذا لـزم هـذا التجسـد العجيـب الـذى مـا هـو فـوق الطبيعـة وذلـك تنفيـذاً للعـدل الالهـى «أن النفـس التـى تخطـئ هـى تمـوت» (عـز١٨: ٢٠)، وعليـه، فقـد إقتضـت رحمـة اللـه أن تقـوم بعمـل التكفـير عـن الانسـان المذنـب. وبذلـك يكـون اللـه عـادلاً ورحيـماً فى آن واحـد. فالعـدل قـد إسـتوفى حقـه بمـوت الابـن عـلى خشـبة الصليـب. والرحمـة قـد توسـطت في صنـع الخـلاص فصـار عـدل اللـه ورحمتـه متسـاويين إذ كل منهـما قـد اسـتوفى حقـه حتـى لا يكـون بينهـما تفـاوت.

The following section was found in an ancient Pascha book:
As for the bodily death of the Lord Christ, its divine sacred superior purposes are great and tremendously auspicious to us, His servants who believe in Him and have hope in His immense favor and His generous gifts. They are:

Reconciling Us with God:
We angered God, His Father, by our evil deeds and our insistence on committing sins and transgressions; hence, a firm punishment and a painful torture precedent, and a partition—a dividing barrier existed between Him and us. The death of the Lord of glory wiped out the handwriting against us, broke down the middle wall separating us from God, removed the enmity, brought us closer to Him, and reconciled us via His cross. St. Paul says, "For it pleased the Father that in Him all the fullness should dwell, and by Him to reconcile all things to Himself, by Him, whether things on earth or things in heaven, having made peace through the blood of His cross" (Col 1:19–20). The Apostle Paul tells the Ephesians, "For He Himself is our peace, who has made both one, and has broken down the middle wall of separation, having abolished in His flesh the enmity, that is, the law of commandments contained in ordinances, so as to create in Himself one new man from the two, thus making peace, and that He might reconcile them both to God in one body through the cross, thereby putting to death the enmity. And He came and preached peace to you who were afar off and to those who were near" (Eph 2:14–17). The apostle also writes to the Romans, "For if when we were enemies we were reconciled to God through the death of His Son, much more, having been reconciled, we shall be saved by His life" (Rom 5:10).

Removing the Curse:
He cleared us of the curse resulting from disobeying and breaking the laws: "Cursed is everyone who does not continue in all things which are written

النبذة التالية وجدت بالبصخة القديمة:

أما موت السيد المسيح بالجسد فكان لغايات مقدسة سامية ومفيدة وعظيمة لنا نحن عبيده المؤمنين بإسمه الراجين عفوه المنشود وفضله العظيم وهى:

مصالحاتنا مع الله:

أولاً- لأننا أغضبنا الله أبيه بسوء أفعالنا وإنصبابنا على إرتكاب المعاصى والآثام، فأعد لنا عقاب صارم وعذاب أليم، وصار بيننا وبينه فاصل وحاجز منيع. فبموت السيد له المجد محا الصك الذى كان مكتوباً علينا، ونقض الحاجز المتوسط، بيننا وبين الله، وأزال العداوة وقربنا منه -له المجد- وصالحنا بصليبه، كما يقول بولس الرسول «لأنه فيه سُرَّ أن يَحِل كل الملء وأن يصالح به الكل لنفسه عاملاً الصلح بدم صليبه بواسطته سواء كان ما على الأرض أم مافى السموات» (كو١: ١٩-٢٠)، وكما يقول أيضاً لأهل أفسس «لأنه هو سلامنا الذى جعل الإثنين واحداً ونقض حائط السياج المتوسط أى العداوة، مبطلاً بجسده ناموس الوصايا فى فرائض لكى يخلق الإثنين فى نفسه إنساناً واحداً جديداً صانعاً سلاماً ويصالح الإثنين في جسد واحد مع الله بالصليب قاتلاً العداوة به. فجاء وبشركم بسلام أنتم البعيدين والقريبين» (أف٢: ١٤-١٧)، وكما يقول لأهل رومية «لأنه وإن متنا ونحن أعداء قد صولحنا مع الله بموت إبنه، فبالأولى كثيراً ونحن مصالحون نخلص بحياته» (رو٥ : ١٠).

رفع اللعنة عنا:

ثانيا- ليبررنا من لعنة الناموس التى حلت عينا من جراء مخافتنا وكسرنا للناموس، كما قيل «ملعون كل من لايثبت فى جميع ماهو مكتوب فى كتاب الناموس ليعمل

in the book of the law, to do them" (Gal 3:10). When no one kept the law, all were accursed; since death on the cross is a curse, He wanted to die the death of the cross to take away our curse, and send us the blessing, as the apostle says, "Christ has redeemed us from the curse of the law, having become a curse for us (for it is written, 'Cursed is everyone who hangs on a tree' (Cf. Deut. 21:22-23)), that the blessing of Abraham might come upon the Gentiles in Christ Jesus, that we might receive the promise of the Spirit through faith" (Gal 3:13–14).

The Life of Righteousness:

So that we might die to sin through His death and live through His life, as St. Peter the Apostle wrote, "Who Himself bore our sins in His own body on the tree, that we, having died to sins, might live for righteousness" (1 Pet 2:24).

Freedom from Slavery:

He died that He might taste the pain of death, abolish it, trample it, crush it, and destroy it, as the writer, the Apostle Paul, to the Hebrews states: "Inasmuch then as the children have partaken of flesh and blood, He Himself likewise shared in the same, that through death He might destroy him who had the power of death, that is, the devil, and release those who through fear of death were all their lifetime subject to bondage" (Heb 2:14–15).

A Copy of a Letter[38]

From Reboleolino, the mayor of Judea in Jerusalem, to the court of Rome's Caesar,[39] this letter was found in the safe of Prince Sharaweeny of Italy, in which he described the appearance and news of the Lord Christ. These are his words:

بـه» (غـل٣: ١٠)، ولما لم يحفـظ أحـد النامـوس صـار الـكل ملعونـين، ولأن مـوت الصليـب لعنـة فأحـب أن يمـوت مـوت الصليـب ليرفـع عنـا اللعنـة، ويرسـل لنـا البركـة كـما يقـول الرسـول «المسـيح إفتدانـا مـن لعنـة النامـوس إذ صـار لعنـة لأجلنـا لأنـه مكتـوب ملعـون كل مـن علـق عـلى خشـبة لتصير بركـة إبراهيـم للأمـم فى المسـيح يسـوع لننـال بالإيمـان موعـد الـروح» (غـل٣: ١٣-١٤).

لكى نحيا للبر:

ثالثـاً- لـكى نمـوت نحـن عـن خطايانـا بموتـه ونحيـا بحياتـه، كـما يقـول بطـرس الرسـول «المسـيح حمـل هـو نفسـه خطايانـا فى جسـده عـلى الخشـبة لـكى نمـوت عـن الخطايـا فنحيـا للـبر» (١بـط٢: ٢٤).

ونعتق من العبودية:

رابعـاً- مـات لـكى يـذوق ألم المـوت ويبطلـه ويدوسـه ويسـحقه ويلاشيه، كـما يقـول كاتـب رسـالة العبرانيـين «فـإذ قـد تشـارك الأولاد فى اللحـم والـدم إشـترك هـو أيضـاً كذلـك فيهـما لـكي يبيـد بالمـوت ذاك الـذى لـه سـلطان المـوت أى إبليس ويعتـق أولئك الذيـن خوفـاً مـن المـوت كانـوا جميعـاً كل حياتهـم تحـت العبوديـة» (عـب٢: ١٤-١٥).

صورة خطاب[٣٨]

مرسـل مـن ربوليولينـو مديـر اليهوديـة بأورشـليم إلى محفـل قيـصر[٣٩] روميـة، وهـذا الخطـاب المذكـور وجـد فى خزانـة الأمير شروينـى مـن ايطاليـا يصـف فيـه شـكل وأخبـار السـيد المسـيح وهـا هـو بحروفـه:

Your majesty, I have learned that you wish to know what I am about to tell you:

There has appeared in our times, and still is, a man of great virtue named Christ Jesus, who is called by the Gentiles a prophet of truth, whom His disciples call the Son of God, raising the dead and healing diseases. He is a man of lofty stature, handsome, having a venerable countenance which the beholders can both love and fear. He has wavy hair, rather crisp, of a tinge, and glossy, flowing down from His shoulders, with a parting in the middle of the head after the manner of the Nazarenes.[40] His forehead is even and very serene, and His face without any wrinkle or spot, and beautiful with a slight blush. His nose and mouth are without fault; He has a beard abundant and reddish, of the color of His hair, not long but forked. His eyes are sparkling and bright. He is terrible in rebuke, calm and loving in admonition, cheerful but preserving gravity, has never been seen to laugh but often to weep. Thus, in stature of body, He is tall; and His hands and limbs are beautiful to look upon. In speech He is grave, reserved, and modest and He is fair among the children of men. He is claimed as the creator of heaven and earth and all that exists therein. Truly, every day we hear amazing news about this Jesus. His appearance overflows with reverence and awe. His eyes are like the rays of the sun, and no one could stare at Him from the brightness of His face. His arms and shoulders are exquisite. As for the meetings, in them he pleases many, yet rarely looks at them, and when He is present with them, He sits with the greatest propriety. So, in His appearance and form, He is the most beautiful person you could imagine, greatly resembling His mother who is the most beautiful young lady to be seen in this area. O king, if your majesty wishes to see Him, please inform me, whereby I will not delay in sending Him to you speedily. He has astonished the whole city of Jerusalem with His knowledge, knowing everything without having studied. Sometimes, He walks barefoot and bareheaded, and many, when they see Him laugh at Him, but in His presence or when speaking

أيها الملك إننى فهمت أنك ترغب معرفة ما أخبرك به الآن.

لأنـه فى وقتنـا هـذا وُجِدَ رجـل عائش عيشـة فاضلـة يدعونه رسـول الفضيلـة، وتلاميذه يقولـون انـه إبـن اللـه خالـق السـماء والأرض وكل مـا يوجـد فيهـما، بالحقيقـة أن كل يـوم نسـمع أمـورا عجيبـة عـن يسـوع هـذا، فهـو يقيـم المـوتى ويشـفى السـقماء بكلمـة واحـدة، وهـو معتـدل القامـة وجميـل المنظـر جـداً، ووجهـه ذو هيبـة هكـذا حتـى أن الذيـن ينظـرون إليـه يشـعرون باجتذابهـم اليـه ويحبـوه ويخافـوه، شـعر رأسـه نـازل لحـد أذنيـه ومـن أذنيـه مسـتدل عـلى كتفيـه، وهـو بلـون الـتراب إنمـا يفـوق عليـه ضيـاء، وفى وسـط جبينـه غـرة كعـادة الناصريـين.[٤٠] أمـا جبينـه فمبسـوط ووجهـه كثـير الصفـاء، ليـس فيـه تجعـد ولا علامـة البتـة. وخـداه فى غايـة الاعتـدال، أنفـه وفمـه لا يقاسـان بحسـن فى أحـد، منظـره يفيـض خشـوعاً، فرحـاً، وورعـاً، عينـاه كأشـعة الشـمس فـلا أحـد يقـدر أن يحـدق بنظـرة اليـه مـن كـثرة الضيـاء. إذا وبـخ أرهـب، إن نصـح أبـكى، ويجعـل الجميـع يحترمونـه لأنـه ذو سـماحة وهيبـة. يقولـون أنـه لم يُنظَـر ضاحـكاً قـط بـل باكيـاً وذراعـاه ويـداه زائدة الجـمال. أمـا فى الاجتماعـات فـيُرضى كثيريـن، ولكـن ينظـر إليهـم نـادراً، وعنـد وجـوده بينهـم يجلـس بغايـة التهذيـب. ففـى رؤيتـه وشـكله هـو أجمـل إنسـان يمكـن تخيلـه، ومشـابه بمقـدار عظيـم لأمِـهِ التـى هـى أجمـل فتـاة يمكـن مشـاهدتها أو تشـاهد قـط بهـذه الجهـات. فيـا أيهـا الملـك إن رغبـت جلالتكـم أن تـراه فاخـبرنى لـكى لا أتقاعـد عـن توجيهـه إليـك سريعـاً. عـلى إنـه بالعلـوم قـد أذهـل مدينـة أورشـليم بأجمعهـا، فهـو يعـرف كافـة العلـوم مـن غـير أن يتعلـم، وتـارة يمـشى حـافى الاقـدام مكشـوف الـرأس كمجنـون، وكثـيرون عنـد نظرهـم اليـه يضحكـون منـه أمـا فى حضـوره أو التكلـم معـه فأنـه يُرهِـب ويُذهِـل، ويقولـون أنـه لم يُسـمع قـط عـن رجـل هكـذا فى الجهـات، وبالحقيقـة مثـل مـا يقـول لى اليهـود إننـا لم نسـمع قـط مشـورات حكمـة مـن أحـد كمثـل مـا يُعلِـم يسـوع هكـذا. وكثـيرون آخـرون يتهكمـون ويشـتكون لى منـه قائلـين أنـه مضـاد لشريعـة عظمتكـم، وتـرانى معنفـاً جـداً مـن هـؤلاء اليهـود الأشرار، ويقولـون إنـه مـا أغـاظ أحـداً قـط بـل كافـة الذيـن عرفـوه وأخـبرونى عنـه يقولـون إنـه حاصـل لهـم منـه إنعامـات وصحـة كثـيرة، وفى كل الأمـور إنى مسـتعد لطاعتكـم ومـن ثـم كل مـا تأمـر بـه جلالتكـم يجـرى.

> to Him, He confounds and astonishes. They say that there has never been heard of such a man in wisdom, and truthfully as the Jews have told me, we have not heard such wisdom from anyone like what this Jesus teaches. Many others come forward complaining to me of Him, saying that He opposes your laws, and you find me very indignant from those evil Jews. They say that He gives them many graces and much health, and in all cases I am ready to obey you; whatever your majesty commands me to do will be done with all speed.

From the Cross to the Tomb

Romans were in the habit of leaving the bodies of those crucified on their crosses, to be eaten by the vultures, wild animals, or to decompose, but the Jews had a stern command from Almighty God that the body shall not hang overnight on the wood (Deut 21:23), but must be brought down and buried the same day of crucifixion.

The Valley of Hinnom

They used to cast the bodies of the dead in a pit in the Valley of Hinnom. This valley bore many names; the part falling southwest of Jerusalem is called Rabbabba Valley; in the Holy Bible it is called Valley of Hinnom (Josh 15:8; Neh 11:30), Valley of the son of Hinnom (Josh 15:8, 18:16), and Valley of the sons of Hinnom (KJV 2 Kg 23:10). It is a valley descending from the Hebron Gate to Job's Well, separating Mount Zion from the Mount of Corruption. The southeastern portion of this valley is called Tophet (Jer 7:31; 2 Kg 23:10), or the Valley of Slaughter (Jer 7:32; 19:6), a border separating Benjamin and Judah. Solomon built on the southern crevice overlooking Tophet, the high places for Moab (1 Kg 11:7). Ahaz (2 Kg 16:3; 2 Chr 28:3) and Manasseh (2 Chr 33:6) passed their children through the fire in this valley. Josiah stopped this worship by desecrating the valley and the high places with human bones and other unclean objects, breaking the sacred pillars, and cutting down the wooden images (2 Kg

إنزال السيد المسيح له المجد عن الصليب ووضعه فى القبر

جرت العادة عند الرومانيين أن يتركوا جثث المصلوبين على صلبانهم حتى تأكلها الجوارح أو وحوش البرية أو تتلاشى من ذاتها. أما اليهود فكان عليهم أمر صريح من الله تعالى ألا تبيت جثة المعلق على الخشبة، بل تُنزل وتُدفن فى ذات اليوم الذي يصلب فيه (تث ٢١: ٢٣).

وادى هنوم:

كانوا يطرحون جثث القتلى فى حفرة فى وادى هنّوم. ويسمى هذا الوادى بعدة أسماء منها الجزء الواقع جنوب غربى أورشليم يدعى «بوادى ربابة». و يسمى فى الكتاب المقدس «وادى هنوم» (يش١٥: ٨)، (نح١١: ٣٠)، و»وادى ابن هنوّم» (يش١٥: ٨، ١٨: ١٦)، و»وادى بنى هنوم» (٢مل٢٣: ١٠)، وهو وادٍ ينحدر من «باب الخليل» إلى «بئر أيوب» ويفصل «جبل صهيون» عن «تل المؤامرة السيئة». ويسمى الجزء الجنوبى الشرقى من هذا الوادى «توفة» (أر٧: ٣١)، (٢مل٢٣: ١٠)، أو «وادى القتل» (أر٧: ٣٢) ، (١٩: ٦) وكان تخماً بين بنيامين ويهوذا. وكان قد بنى سليمان على الجرف الجنوبى المشرف عليه مرتفعات لموآب (١مل١١: ٧)، وهو الذى أجاز فيه آحاز ومنسى أولادهما بالنار (٢مل١٦: ٣)، (٢أخ٢٨: ٣، ٣٣: ٦) فى هذا الوادى، وفيه أيضاً أبطل يوشيا هذه العبادة بتنجيسه الوادى والمرتفعات بعظام الناس وباشياء أخرى دنسه، وبتكسيره التماثيل، وقطعه السوارى (٢مل٢٣: ١٠، ١٣، ١٤) ومن ثم صار متغوطاً

23:10,13,14). It became a place where all of the city's rubbish was thrown out, and into where the entire city's cesspool poured. Looking at what defiled this valley: Molech's fire, and the fire used to burn the rubbish, the Jews took to calling it Gehinnom [Hades] (land of Hinnom), making it a general location for punishment, throwing the bodies of the two thieves there. Had Joseph not come forward, asking Pilate for the body of the Lord Jesus, He would have been thrown with the thieves, as the Jewish rulers intended.

Embalming Jesus

Joseph took the body, aided by Nicodemus, who followed him, being a Sanhedrin council member, coming with 100 pounds of spices, a mixture of myrrh and aloes. Nicodemus supported Joseph in opposition to the ruling which the Jews passed against Jesus (Jn 7:50–52). They wrapped Him in pure linen which was only done by the rich, noble, and affluent. The linen was a long strip to be wrapped around the body several times. No doubt the spices were placed on the body, mingling with it, and then He was wrapped in the strip and placed in the tomb. As Almighty God previously appointed Joseph the carpenter to care for Jesus during His childhood, He now appointed another Joseph to bury Him.

This reminds us of another Joseph, the son of Jacob in the Old Testament, who provided food for the people of Israel in Egypt.

His Burial

Here, we again see God's mighty care. It was not in the means of the Virgin Mary or the disciples to take the body, but Joseph, who was unknown at that time as a disciple, but as a rich noble man, took it with the greatest ease. Thus, Isaiah's prophecy was fulfilled: "And they made His grave with the wicked—but with the rich at His death" (Is 53:9). Also, Nicodemus, who came to learn from Jesus three years earlier (Jn 3:2), appeared now

تنصب اليه بواليع البلد ومرمى كناساتها. وبالنظر إلى ما تنجس به هذا الوادى من «نار مولك» ومن «النيران المستعملة لاحراق الكناسات»، أخذ اليهود يسمونه جهنم (أى أرض هنّوم)، وجعلوه علماً لموضع العقاب، وفيه طرحت جثتا اللصين. ولولا أن يوسف تقدم إلى بيلاطس وطلب جسد الرب يسوع لطرح مع اللصين كما كان قصد رؤساء اليهود.

تكفين يسوع:

فأخذ يوسف الجسد وساعده على ذلك نيقوديموس الذى يماثله لكونه من أعضاء مجلس السبعين، وهو أيضاً كان يوافق يوسف فى الرأى إذ لم يكن موافقاً على الحكم الذى أصدره اليهود ضد يسوع (يو٧: ٥٠-٥٢). هذا أتى بمئة رطل طيب من مزيج المر والعود. ولفاه بكتان نقى، وهذا لايفعله إلا الاغنياء والشرفاء وذوى المقامات الرفيعة. وكان ذلك الكتان شقة طويلة تلف علي الجسم جملة مرات، ولابد من أن الاطياب وُضعت على الجسم وضُمخ بها وبعد ذلك لُف باللفافة ووضع فى القبر. فكما ان لله تعالى قد عين قبلاً «يوسف النجار» ليعتنى بيسوع فى طفوليته. قد عين الآن «يوسفاً» أخر ليدفنه.

وهذا يذكرنا «بيوسف بن يعقوب» فى العهد القديم الذى أعد القوت لشعب إسرائيل فى مصر.

دفنه:

وهنا نرى أيضاً عناية الله العظيمة، فأنه لم يكن فى وسع السيدة مريم العذراء ولا التلاميذ أن يأخذوا الجسد، ولكن «يوسف» الذى لم يكن يُعرف فى ذلك الوقت كتلميذ، بل كانسان غنى ومشير، أخذه بغاية السهولة وتمت نبوة أشعياء «جعل مع الأشرار قبره ومع غنى عند موته» (أش٥٣: ٩)، ثم ان نيقوديموس الذى أتى إلى يسوع

accompanying Joseph and helped him in the preparations for burying the Savior. He was placed in a new tomb, in which no one had been placed before, because God had ordained that the One who would not see corruption would not be placed in a tomb with other corrupted bodies (Ps 16:10; Acts 2:31). How amazing are God's care and economy!

Three Days and Three Nights

The Lord's body was placed in the tomb on Friday before sunset, and rose in the early dawn of Sunday. Thus, the time in which the Lord slept in the tomb was about 36 hours: part of Friday, Saturday (all day and night), and part of Sunday when He rose early. This duration is considered three days and three nights; this is a principle in the Talmud, such that adding one hour to a day counts as another day, and adding a day to a year counts as another year. The same principle was applied in Book of Esther (Esth 4:15–16), and this applies even today in our government. Most governments count one day of the year, a full year. For example, if a child is born on the last day of the year, the whole year is counted for him. Therefore, it is valid to say that the Lord Christ stayed in the tomb for three days and three nights, otherwise the Jews would have objected to the Christians and challenged the veracity of Christ for not fulfilling His promise of rising on the morning of the third day, but they never presented such an objection.

قبـل الآن بثـلاث سـنين لـكى يتعلـم منـه (يـو٣: ٢)، ظهـر وقتئـذ أيضـاً كصديـق ليوسـف وسـاعده فى الاسـتعدادات لدفـن المخلـص لـه المجـد. وقـد وضـع فى قـبر جديـد لم يوضـع فيه أحـد، لان اللـه قـد عـين أن الـذى لا يـرى الفسـاد لا يوضـع فى قـبر مـع أجسـاد أخـرى تفسـد (مـز١٦: ١٠)، (أع٢: ٣١). فـما أعجـب عنايـة اللـه وتدبـيره.

ثلاثة أيام وثلاثة ليال:

إن جسـد الـرب قـد وضِـعَ فى القـبر يـوم الجمعـة قبـل غـروب الشـمس، وقـام لـه المجـد فى صبـاح الأحـد باكـرا، فتكـون المـدة التـى نامهـا السـيد في القـبر نحـو سـت وثلاثـين سـاعة، جـزء مـن يـوم الجمعـة، ويـوم السـبت بليلـه، وجـزء مـن يـوم الأحـد الـذى قـام فيـه باكـراً. فقـد تُعتـبر هـذه المـدة ثـلاث أيـام وثـلاث ليـال، وذلـك مبـدأ فى كتـاب التلمـود الـذى يُعـد أقـدس كتـاب عنـد اليهـود بعـد كتـاب اللـه. وهـو إن اضافـه سـاعة إلى يـوم تُحسـب يومـاً آخـر وإضافـه يـوم إلى سـنة يُحسـب سـنة أخـرى. وكـذا كان الامـر فى أسـتير (أس ٤: ١٥-١٦)، وهكـذا يجـرى هـذا الاصطـلاح لوقتنـا هـذا فى حكومتنـا، وجميـع الحكومـات، تحسـب يومـاً واحـداً مـن السـنة سـنة كاملـة. مثـلا إذا ولـد طفـل فى آخـر يـوم مـن السـنة، تحسـب لـه السـنة كلهـا. وعـلى ذلـك فأنـه قـد يصـح القـول بـأن السـيد المسـيح قـد مكـث فى القـبر ثـلاث أيـام وثـلاث ليـال. ولـولا ذلـك لاعـترض اليهـود عـلى المسـيحيين وادعـوا كـذب مسـيحهم لعـدم اتمـام وعـده بقيامتـه صبـاح اليـوم الثالـث. ولكنهـم لم يأتـوا هـذا الاعـتراض بالمـرة.

Bright Saturday

باكر يوم سبت الفرح

Romans were in the habit of leaving the bodies of those crucified on their crosses, to be eaten by the vultures, wild animals, or to decompose, but the Jews had a stern command from Almighty God that the body shall not hang overnight on the wood (Deut 21:23), but must be brought down and buried the same day of crucifixion.

جرت العادة عند الرومانيين أن يتركوا جثث المصلوبين علي صلبانهم حتي تأكلهم الجوارح أو حيوانات البرية أو تتلاشي من ذاتها، أما اليهود فكان عليهم أمر صريح من الله تعالي ألا تبيت جثة المعلق علي الخشبة، بل تُنْزَل وتُدْفَن في ذات اليوم الذي يصلب فيه (تث٢١:٢٣). وكانوا يطرحون جثث القتلي في حفرة في وادي هنوم.

The Valley of Hinnom

They used to cast the bodies of the dead in a pit in the Valley of Hinnom. This valley bore many names; the part falling southwest of Jerusalem is called Rabbabba Valley; in the Holy Bible it is called Valley of Hinnom (Josh 15:8; Neh 11:30), Valley of the son of Hinnom (Josh 15:8, 18:16), and Valley of the sons of Hinnom (KJV 2 Kg 23:10). It is a valley descending from the Hebron Gate to Job's Well,

وادى هنوم:

يسمي هذا الوادي بعدة أسماء، منها الجزء الواقع جنوب غربي أورشليم يدعي «بوادي ربابة»، ويسمي في الكتاب المقدس «وادي هنوم» (يش ٨:١٥)، (نح١١:٣٠)، ووادي ابن هنوم (يش١٥:٨ ، ١٨:١٦)، ووادي بي هنوم (٢مل٢٣ : ١٠)، وهو وادٍ ينحدر من باب الخليل الي بئر أيوب ويفصل

separating Mount Zion from the Mount of Corruption. The southeastern portion of this valley is called Tophet (Jer 7:31; 2 Kg 23:10), or the Valley of Slaughter (Jer 7:32; 19:6), a border separating Benjamin and Judah. Solomon built on the southern crevice overlooking Tophet, the high places for Moab (1 Kg 11:7). Ahaz (2 Kg 16:3; 2 Chr 28:3) and Manasseh (2 Chr 33:6) passed their children through the fire in this valley. Josiah stopped this worship by desecrating the valley and the high places with human bones and other unclean objects, breaking the sacred pillars, and cutting down the wooden images (2 Kg 23:10,13,14). It became a place where all of the city's rubbish was thrown out, and into where the entire city's cesspool poured. Looking at what defiled this valley: Molech's fire, and the fire used to burn the rubbish, the Jews took to calling it Gehinnom [Hades] (land of Hinnom), making it a general location for punishment, throwing the bodies of the two thieves there. Had Joseph not come forward, asking Pilate for the body of the Lord Jesus, He would have been thrown with the thieves, as the Jewish rulers intended.

Embalming Jesus

Joseph took the body, aided by Nicodemus, who followed him, being a Sanhedrin council member, coming with 100 pounds of spices, a mixture of myrrh and aloes. Nicodemus supported Joseph in opposition to the ruling which the Jews passed against Jesus (Jn 7:50–52). They wrapped Him in pure linen which was only done by the rich, noble, and affluent. The linen was a long strip to be wrapped around the body several times. No doubt the spices were placed on the body, mingling with it, and then He was wrapped in the strip and placed in the tomb. As Almighty God previously appointed Joseph the carpenter to care for Jesus during His childhood, He now appointed another Joseph to bury Him.

This reminds us of another Joseph, the son of Jacob in the Old Testament, who provided food for the people of Israel in Egypt.

جبل صهيون عن تل المؤامرة السيئة. ويسمي الجزء الجنوبي الشرقي من هذا الوادي «توفة» (ار٧ : ٣١) ، (٢مل٢٣: ١٠) أو «وادي القتل» (ار٣٢:٧ ، ٦:١٩) وكان تُخماً بين بنيامين ويهوذا، وبني سليمان علي الجرف الجنوبي المشرف عليه «مرتفعات لموآب» (١مل١١:٧)، وأجاز آحاز ومنسي أولادهما بالنار في هذا الوادي (٢ مل ٣:١٦)، (٢اخ ٣:٢٨ ،٦:٣٣)، وأبطل يوشيا هذه العبادة بتنجيسه الوادي والمرتفعات بعظام الناس وبأشياء أخر دنسه، وبتكسيره التماثيل، وقطعه السواري (٢مل٢٣:١٠، ١٣ ،١٤)، (٢اي٣٤:٤ ،٥). ومن ثم صار متغوطاً تنصبُّ اليه بواليع البلد ومرمي كناساتها. وبالنظر الي ما تنجس به هذا الوادي من نار مولك ومن ثم بالنيران المستعملة لإحراق الكناسات، أخذ اليهود يسمونه جهنم (أي أرض هنوم)، وجعلوه عَلَماً لموضع العقاب، وفيه طُرِحت جثتا اللصين. ولولا أن يوسف تقدم الي بيلاطس وطلب جسد الرب يسوع، لطُرِحٍ مع اللصين وهذا ما كان يقصده رِؤساء اليهود.

تحنيط جسد يسوع:

أخذ يوسف الجسد وساعده علي ذلك نيقوديموس الذي يماثله في كونه من أعضاء مجلس السبعين. وهذا أتي بمئة رطل طيب من مزيج المر والعود. وهو أيضا كان يوافق يوسف في الرأي ولَم يكن موافقا علي الحُكم الذي أصدره اليهود ضد يسوع (يو٧:٥٠-٥٢)، ولفاه بكتان نقي، وهذا لا يفعله إلا الأغنياء والشرفاء وذوي المقامات الرفيعة. وكان ذلك الكتان شقة طويلة تلف علي الجسم جملة مرات ولابد من أن الأطياب وُضِعتْ علي الجسم، وضُمِخ بها، وبعد ذلك لُفَ باللفافة، ووُضعَ في القبر. فكما أن الله تعالي قد عَينَ قبلاً يوسف النجار ليعتني بيسوع في طفولته، قد عَينَ الآن يوسفاً أخر ليدفنه.

وهذا يُذكرنا بيوسف بن يعقوب في العهد القديم الذي أعدَ القوت لشعب إسرائيل في مصر.

His Burial

Here, we again see God's mighty care. It was not in the means of the Virgin Mary or the disciples to take the body, but Joseph, who was unknown at that time as a disciple, but as a rich noble man, took it with the greatest ease. Thus, Isaiah's prophecy was fulfilled: "And they made His grave with the wicked—but with the rich at His death" (Is 53:9). Also, Nicodemus, who came to learn from Jesus three years earlier (Jn 3:2), appeared now accompanying Joseph and helped him in the preparations for burying the Savior. He was placed in a new tomb, in which no one had been placed before, because God had ordained that the One who would not see corruption would not be placed in a tomb with other corrupted bodies (Ps 16:10; Acts 2:31). How amazing are God's care and economy!

Three Days and Three Nights

The Lord's body was placed in the tomb on Friday before sunset, and rose in the early dawn of Sunday. Thus, the time in which the Lord slept in the tomb was about 36 hours: part of Friday, Saturday (all day and night), and part of Sunday when He rose early. This duration is considered three days and three nights; this is a principle in the Talmud, such that adding one hour to a day counts as another day, and adding a day to a year counts as another year. The same principle was applied in Book of Esther (Esth 4:15–16), and this applies even today in our government. Most governments count one day of the year, a full year. For example, if a child is born on the last day of the year, the whole year is counted for him. Therefore, it is valid to say that the Lord Christ stayed in the tomb for three days and three nights, otherwise the Jews would have objected to the Christians and challenged the veracity of Christ for not fulfilling His promise of rising on the morning of the third day, but they never presented such an objection.

دفنه:

وهنـا نـري أيضـاً عنايـة اللـه العظيمـة فإنـه لم يكـن في وُسـِعْ السـيدة مريـم العـذراء ولا التلاميـذ أن يأخـذوا الجسـد، ولكـن يوسـف الـذي لم يكـن يُعـرَف في ذلـك الوقـت كتلميـذ بـل كإنسـان غنـي ومشـير، أخـذه بغايـة السـهولة وتمـت نبـوة أشـعياء «جُعِـلَ مـع الأشرار قـبره ومـع غنـي عنـد موتـه» (آش ٩:٥٣)، ثـم أن نيقوديمـوس الـذي أتي الي يسـوع قَبِـلَ الآن بثـلاث سـنين لـكي يتعلـم منـه (يـو٢:٣)، ظهـر وقتئـْذٍ أيضـا كصديـق ليوسـف وسـاعده في الإسـتعدادات لدفـن المخلـص لـه المجـد. وقـد وُضِـعَ في قـبرٍ جديـد لم يوضـع فيـه أحـد لان اللـه قـد عـيّن أن الـذي لا يـري الفسـاد لا يوضـع في قـبر مـع أجسـاد أخـري تفسـد (مـز١٦:١٠)، (أع ٣١:٢). فـما أعجـب عنايـة اللـه وتدبـيره.

ثلاث أيام وثلاث ليال:

أن جسـد الـرب قـد وُضـع في القـبر يـوم الجمعـة قبـل غـروب الشـمس، وقـام في صبـاح الأحـد باكـراً، فتكـون المـدة التـي نامهـا السـيد في القـبر نحـو سـتٍ وثلاثـين سـاعة، فهـى جـزء مـن يـوم الجمعـة، وجـزء مـن يـوم السـبت بليلـه، وجـزء مـن يـوم الأحـد الـذي قـام فيـه باكـراً. فقـد تُعتـبر هـذه المـدة ثـلاث أيـام وثـلاث ليـالٍ. وذلـك مبـدأ في كتـاب التلمـود الـذي يُعـد أقـدس كتـاب عنـد اليهـود بعـد كتـاب اللـه، وهـو أن إضافـة سـاعة إليّ يـوم تُحسـب يومـاً آخـر، وإضافـة يـوم إليّ سـنة يُحسـب سـنة أخـري. وكـذا كان الأمـر في أسـتير (آش ١٦:٤ ، ١٥)، وهكـذا جـارٍ هـذا الإصطـلاح لوقتنـا هـذا في حكومتنـا السـنِية وجميـع الحكومـات إذ تَحسِـب يومـاً واحـداً مـن السـنة سـنة كاملـة. فمثـلا لـو وُلِـدَ الطفـل في آخـر يـوم مـن السـنة تُحسـب لـه السـنة كلهـا. وعـلي ذلـك فانـه قـد صـح القـول بـأن السـيد المسـيح قـد مكـث في القـبر ثلاثـة أيـام وثـلاث ليـالٍ. ولـولا ذلـك لإعـترض اليهـود عـلي المسـيحين وإدعـوا كـذِب مسـيحهم لعـدم إتمـام وعـده بقيامتـه صبـاح اليـوم الثالـث. ولكنهـم لم يأتـوا هـذا الإعـتراض بالمـرة.

Reasons for Christ's Death

The death of the Lord Christ in the flesh was for very sacred, sublime, helpful, and grand purposes for us, His faithful servants who hope for and seek His forgiveness and deep favor:

The first purpose is to reconcile us with God His Father, whom we had angered by our vile deeds and insistence on committing transgressions. Thus, He had prepared for us severe punishment, painful torment, and an impenetrable barrier separating us from God. Through the death of the Master, to whom is due glory, He blotted out the writing against us, broke the middle barrier between us and God, removed the enmity, brought us closer to Him, and reconciled us through His cross, as the Apostle Paul says, "For it pleased the Father that in Him all the fullness should dwell, and by Him to reconcile all things to Himself, by Him, whether things on earth or things in heaven, having made peace through the blood of His cross" (Col 1:19-20). The same apostle also says in his letter to the Ephesians, "For He Himself is our peace, who has made both one, and has broken down the middle wall of separation, having abolished in His flesh the enmity, that is, the law of commandments contained in ordinances, so as to create in Himself one new man from the two, thus making peace, and that He might reconcile them both to God in one body through the cross, thereby putting to death the enmity. And He came and preached peace to you who were afar off and to those who were near" (Eph 2:14-17). And also saying to the Romans, "For if when we were enemies we were reconciled to God through the death of His Son, much more, having been reconciled, we shall be saved by His life" (Rom 5:10).

The second purpose is to justify us from the curse of the law that had befallen us as a result of our breach and disobedience to the law, as it is written, "Cursed is everyone who does not continue in all things which are written in the book of the law, to do them" (Gal 3:10). Everyone broke the law, and therefore, everyone became accursed. When death by the cross was installed as a curse, God wanted to die on the cross to lift off the curse from upon us, and to send us the blessing. The Apostle Paul says, "Christ

سبب موت المسيح:

أما موت السيد المسيح بالجسد فكان لغايةٍ، مقدسةٍ، ساميةٍ، مفيدةٍ وعظيمةٍ جداً لنا نحن عبيده المؤمنين بإسمه الراجين عفوه المنشود وفضله العميم:

أولاً: ليُصالحنا مع الله أبيه الذي قد أغضبناه بسوء أفعالنا وإنصبابنا علي إرتكاب المعاصي والآثام، وبذا فقد أعد لنا عقاباً صارماً وعذاباً أليماً وصار بيننا وبين الله فاصل وحاجز منيع، فبموت السيد له المجد محا الصك الذي كانَ مكتوباً علينا، ونقض الحاجز المتوسط بيننا وبين الله، وأزال العداوة، وقربنا منه تعالي، وصالحنا بصليبه كما يقول بولس الرسول «لأنه فيه سُرَّ أن يحل كل الملء. وأن يُصالِح به الكلَّ لنفسِهِ، عاملاً الصُلحَ بدمِ صليبِهِ بواسطته، سواء كانَ ما علي الأرض أم ما في السموات» (كو١:١٩، ٢٠)، وكما يقول أيضاً لأهل أفسس «لأنه هو سلامُنا الذي جَعلَ الاثنين واحداً، ونقضَ حائط السياج المتوسط، أي العداوة. مبطلاً بجسده ناموس الوصايا في فرائض، لكي يخلُق الإثنين في نفسهِ إنساناً واحداً جديداً، صانعاً سلاماً، ويصالح الإثنين في جسدٍ واحدٍ مع الله بالصليب قاتلاً العداوة به. فجاءَ وبشركم بسلامٍ أنتم البعيدين والقريبين (اف ٢:١٤-١٧)، وكما يقول لأهل رومية «لأنه إن كنّا ونحن أعداء قد صُولِحنا مع الله بِموتِ إبنهِ فبالأولي كثيراً ونحن مُصالَحون نخلصُ بِحياتِهِ» (رو٥ : ١٠).

ثانياً: ليُبررنا من لعنة الناموس التي حلت علينا من جراء مخالفتنا، وكَسْرِنا للناموس كما قيل «ملعون كل من لا يثبُتْ في جميع ما هو مكتوب في كتاب الناموس ليعْمَل به» (غلا٣:١٠) ولما لم يَحفظ أحد الناموس صار الكل ملعونين، ولما كان موت الصليب لعنة، فأحب الله أن يموت موت الصليب ليرفع عنا اللعنة، ويُرسل لنا البركة كما يقول الرسول «المسيح إفتدانا من لعنة الناموس، إذ صار لعنة لأجلنا، لأنه مكتوب: ملعون كل من عُلِق علي خشبة. لتصير بركة إبراهيم للأمم في المسيح يسوع، لننال بالإيمان موعد الروح» (غل٣:١٣ ، ١٤).

has redeemed us from this curse of the law, having become a curse for us (for it is written, 'Cursed is everyone who hangs on a tree'), that the blessing of Abraham might come upon the Gentiles in Christ Jesus, that we might receive the promise of the Spirit through faith" (Gal 3:13-14).

The third purpose is that we may die to our sins by His death, and live through His life, as the Apostle Peter says, "Who Himself bore our sins in His own body on the tree, that we, having died to sins, might live for righteousness" (1 Pet 2:24).

The fourth purpose is He died that He might taste the pain of death, and nullify, trample, crush, and eliminate it, as the writer Paul of the Epistle to the Hebrews says, "Inasmuch then as the children have partaken of flesh and blood, He Himself likewise shared in the same, that through death He might destroy him who had the power of death, that is, the devil, and release those who through fear of death were all their lifetime subject to bondage" (Heb 2:14-15).

ثالثاً: لكي نموت نحن عن خطايانا بموته ونحيا بحياته كما يقول بطرس الرسول «الذى حَمَلَ هو نفسه خطايانا في جسده علي الخشبة، لكي نموت عن الخطايا فنحيا للبر» (١ بط ٢:٢٤).

رابعاً: مات لكي يذوق ألم الموت ويُبطِله ويدوسه ويسحقه ويلاشيه، كما يقول كاتب رسالة العبرانيين «فإذا قد تَشَارك الأولاد في اللحم والدم إشترك هو أيضاً كذلك فيهما، لكي يبيد بالموت ذاك الذي له سلطان الموت، أي إبليس، ويُعتق أولئك الذين خوفاً من الموت كانوا جميعاً كل حياتهم تحت العبودية» (عب٢:١٤ ، ١٥).

RESURRECTION SUNDAY

باكر يوم أحد القيامة المقدسة

The Resurrection

The Savior, to whom is due all glory, rose from the dead at dawn of the first day of the week, a Sabbath Sunday. "There was a great earthquake; for an angel of the Lord descended from heaven, and came and rolled back the stone from the door [of the tomb], and sat on it" (Mt 28:2). The guards shook with fear, trembling, and alarmed, becoming as dead men, from the awe of the angel.

When that day's dawn began to emerge, the women (Mary Magdalene, Mary the mother of James, Joanna, Salome, and others who had served Him) came to the tomb bearing spices to continue embalming the body of the Lord Jesus, not having finished on Friday because of the hurried burial. "They said among themselves, 'Who will roll away the stone from the door of the tomb for us?'" (Mk 16:3). When they reached the tomb, "they saw that the stone had been rolled away" (Mk 16:4), and that the Lord had

حدث القيامة:

إن مخلصنا لـه المجـد قـد قـام مـن بـين الأمـوات في فجـر اليـوم الأول مـن الإسـبوع. الـذي يدعـي أحـد السـبوت. وإذا زلزلـة عظيمـة قـد حدثـت. لأن مـلاك الـرب نـزل مـن السـماء ودحـرج الحجـر عـن بـاب القـبر وجلـس فوقـه (مـت٢٨: ٢) فَحَصَـل للحـراس خـوف وجَـزَع وإرتعـاد وصـاروا كأمـوات مـن هيبـة المـلاك.

ولما كان فجـر ذلـك اليـوم قـد لاح، خرجـت النسـاء اللـواتي كُـنَ يخدمنـه. أي مريـم المجدليـة ومريـم أم يعقـوب ويونـا وسـالومة وغيرهـن، ومعهـن حنـوط إليّ القـبر لـكي يُكملـن تحنيـط جسـد الـرب يسـوع، لأنـه لم يكمُـل يـوم الجمعـة بسـبب السرعـة في دفنـه. وكُـن يقُلـن فيـما بينهـن. مـن يدحـرج لنـا الحجـر عـن فـم القـبر (مـر١٦: ٣). ولما بلغـن الي القـبر وجـدن أن الحجـر قـد

risen. They were shocked, not knowing anything about the resurrection, about the guards who were sent on Friday to guard the tomb after they had left, or about the seal on the tomb. When they entered the tomb and did not find the body of the Lord, they were greatly perplexed.

When Mary Magdalene saw this, she assumed that the body of the Lord had been stolen, so she left the tomb and all the women who were with her and ran to the city to inform Peter and John. The rest of the women remained at the tomb to verify this occurrence. Promptly, two angels appeared to them and informed them that Jesus had risen from the dead; "He is not here" (Lk 24:6), as they had assumed, and to relay this information to His disciples. They left the tomb quickly and ran speedily towards the city to tell the disciples the events concerning the two angels whom they saw while in the tomb. As they went, they met Jesus on the road, so they "held Him by the feet" (Mt 28:9). He commanded them to tell His disciples the news of His resurrection from the dead, and that they had seen Him on the road. When they "told these things to the apostles... their words seemed to them like idle tales, and they did not believe them" (Lk 24:10-11).

Meanwhile, Peter and John had come from the city with Mary Magdalene, and entering the tomb, they had found it empty. When John saw that the linen cloths, which had been on the body of the Lord, were arranged in one place, and that the handkerchief, which was on His holy head was set aside separately, he was convinced that the body was not taken from there, neither by violence, nor by the hands of friends. The Lord had risen on His own, as He had foretold them, because He has "power to lay it down, and... power to take it again" (Jn 10:18). These two disciples returned to the city, "But Mary stood outside by the tomb weeping, and as she wept she stooped down and looked into the tomb. And she saw two angels in white sitting, one at the head and the other at the feet, where the body of Jesus had lain... she turned around and saw Jesus" (Jn 20:11-14). He spoke with her and commanded her to inform His disciples (Cf. Jn 20:11-20).

دحرج (مر١٦: ٤) والرب قد قام. وقد إندهشنَ إذ لم يعرفن شيئاً عما حدث من أمر القيامة، والحراس الذين أُرسِلوا يوم الجمعة لحراسة القبر بعد غيابهن، ولا مِن أَمَر خَتم القبر. فلما دخلن القبر ولَم يجدن جسد الرب تحيرن جداً.

أما مريم المجدلية فلما رأت ذلك ظنت أن جسد الرب قد سُرق، فتركت القبر وجميع النساء اللواتي كن معها وركضت الي المدينة لكي تُخبر بطرس ويوحنا بذلك. فبقين بقية النساء في القبر ليتحققن من وقوع تلك الحادثة. وللوقت ظهر لهن ملاكان وأخبرهن بأن يسوع قد قام من بين الأموات وليس هو ههنا كما تظنون (لو٢٤: ٦)، وأعلمهُن أن يُبلغن ذلك لتلاميذه. فخرجن من القبر سريعاً وذهبن بسرعة متناهية الي المدينة ليخبرن التلاميذ عما حدث لهن فى أثناء وجودهن في القبر بواسطة الملاكين. وإذا هُن سائرات قد لقاهن يسوع في الطريق فأمسكن بقدميه (مت٢٨: ٩) فأوصاهن بتبليغ رسله خبر قيامته من الأموات، وإنهن قد رأينه في الطريق. ولما توجهن وأخبرن الرسل بهذا كله ترآي كلامهن لهم كالهذيان ولَم يصدقوهن (لو٢٤: ١٠-١١).

وفي أثناء ذلك كان بطرس ويوحنا قد جاءا من المدينة مع مريم المجدلية ودخلا القبر فوجداه خالياً ولكن لما رأي يوحنا أن الأكفان التي كانت علي جسد الرب موضوعة وحدها بالترتيب، وأن المنديل الذي كان علي رأسِهِ المقدسة موضوع أيضا في موضع علي حدته. إقتنع بأن الجسد لم يؤخذ من هناك لا بعنف ولا بأيدي الأصحاب. بل أن الرب قد قام من تلقاء ذاته كما سبق وأخبرهم. لأنه تبارك وتعالي له سلطان أن يضع نفسه وله سلطان أن يأخذها. ثم رجع هذان التلميذان الي المدينة، وأما مريم المجدلية فبقيت واقفة أمام القبر تبكي، وفيما هي تبكي إنحنت ونظرت الي القبر فرأت ملاكين جالسين واحد عند الرأس والآخر عند الرجلين، حيث كان جسد الرب يسوع موضوعاً. ثم إلتفتت إلي الوراء فنظرت يسوع (يو٢٠: ١١-١٤)، وأوصاها أيضاً أن تُخبر التلاميذ بما رأت (يو٢٠: ١١-٢٠).

Meanwhile, "some of the guard came into the city and reported to the chief priests all the things that had happened" (Mt 28:11). This is evidence that the guards were dispersed from the intensity of their fear, and from the resurrection, causing some to go in one direction, while others went into another. Furthermore, leaving the tomb without permission subjected them to severe retribution. This proves the truth of the resurrection, because they could not escape and expose themselves to such punishment, except if they were terribly petrified beyond measure.

Here, we have two groups of reporters. First, the women, and their report was good news to the disciples. Second, we have the guards, and their news was a warning, a cause of sorrow, shame, and upheaval for the chief priests, because they were Christ's enemies who caused His crucifixion.

Attempts to Conceal the Truth of the Resurrection

The Sadducees were most disturbed, because they "say that there is no resurrection" (Acts 23:8). Christ's resurrection became a refutation to their principles. The chief priests had said they would believe in the Savior if He came down from the cross; now they must believe in what is greater than coming down from the cross, as testified by their own guards. They had asked for a sign from the Almighty; He fulfilled His promise to them with the sign of Jonah. They should have repented and believed in Him, according to their request; they never did.

The chief priests and the elders gathered together, the Sanhedrin met, yet not all of its members, but only those who agreed to kill Christ. Without a doubt, Joseph of Arimathea and Nicodemus did not convene with them. The members consulted until they reached an agreement to give the guard a large sum of money—a sufficient bribe. It is no secret that a bribe blinds the hearts of the sighted. They had already bribed Iscariot and the false witnesses before the crucifixion. They were forced after the crucifixion to bribe the guards with even more, instructing and compelling them to

ثم أنه في أثناء ذلك ذهب قوم من الحراس إلي المدينة وأخبروا رؤساء الكهنة بكل ما كان (مت٢٨: ١١). وهذا دليل علي أن الحراس تشتتوا من شدة الخوف الذي لحقهم ومن حادثة القيامة. فذهب بعضهم إلي جهة والبعض الآخر إلي جهة اخري. ثم إن بتركهم القبر بدون إذن عرضهم للقصاص الشديد. وهذا مما يُثبت صحة القيامة. لأنه لا يمكن أن يهربوا ويعرضوا أنفسهم لذلك القصاص إلا لهول عظيم وإضطرار شديد.

وقد ظهر في ذلك فرقتان من المخبرين: الأولي: النساء، وكان خبرهُن بشارة للتلاميذ. الثانية: الحراس، وكان خبرهُم إنذاراً وعلة حزنٍ وخجلٍ للرؤساء وإنزعاجٍ كثير لأنهم أعداء للمسيح وهم السبب في صلبه.

محاولة إخفاء حقيقة القيامة:

وقد أقلق الصدوقيين منهم أكثر مما أزعج جملتهم لأنهم كانوا ينكرون القيامة (اع ٢٣: ٨). وقيامة السيد المسيح قد صارت دحضا لمبدأهم. وكان الرؤساء قد قالوا أن يؤمنوا بالمخلص له المجد إذا نزل عن الصليب. فوجب أن يؤمنوا به لما هو أعظم من النزول عن الصليب بشهادة حراسهم. وهم كانوا قد طلبوا آية منه تعالي فأنجز وعده لهم بآية يونان، فكان الواجب عليهم أن يتوبوا ويؤمنوا به حسب طلبهم، ولكنهم لم يفعلوا شيئاً من ذلك.

فإجتمع رؤساء الكهنة مع الشيوخ وكان ذلك إجتماع مجمع السبعين، لكن ليس كل أعضائه بل المتفقون علي قتل المسيح. ولاشك في أن يوسف الرامي ونيقوديموس لم يجتمعا معهم . فتشاور بعضهم مع بعض حتي إتفقوا علي رأي، وهو أن يعطوا العسكر فضة كثيرة، أي يرشوهم رشوة وافرة. ولا يُخفي أن الرشوة تَعمي قلوب المبصرين. وكانوا قد رشوا الإسخريوطي والشهود الزُّور قبل الصلب. وإضطروا بعد الصلب ان يرشوا العسكر بأكثر من ذلك. مع تفهيمهم وإلزامهم أن يقولوا أن تلاميذه

say that the disciples had come at night and stolen Jesus Christ away while they slept, and to conceal the news of the appearance of the two angels. If the people found out of the appearance of angels, and all the resurrection events, they would definitely believe in the truth of Christ's call, and realize the slanderous lies of the chief priests against the Savior.

Nullifying their Hypocrisy

This revealed their deficiency, their disappointment, and their bewilderment, because they could not reach their goals with more reasonable logic.

What logical person would believe that His disciples, who were fishermen from Galilee, would dare open a tomb guarded by Roman guards? If we assume that they would dare, would they have any hope of success? They would never expect all those guards to be sleeping at the same time, knowing that the punishment for sleeping on duty is death.

What further invalidates their argument is that, if all the guards truly were asleep, how would they know if it was the disciples, or others, who stole Him away? Then, they are cornered into saying that they slept and awoke to find the tomb open and the corpse gone.

If some of them were sleeping while others were keeping watch, as is regular protocol for guards, the ones keeping watch would have alerted the sleepers and prevented the disciples from the theft.

If it were true that the guards had slept, allowing the disciples to steal the body, the disciples would not have left the linen cloths in the tomb, but would have carried Him with His cloths. What is the point of removing His linen cloths and taking Him naked, and then spreading the false report of His resurrection?

Why were the chief priests not angry with the guards, or rush to Pilate to complain about them and demand retribution, and seek their arrest and

قد أتوا ليلاً وسرقوه ونحن نيام. وأن يخفوا حقيقة ظهور الملاكين عن الشعب. لأنه لو عرف الشعب بظهور الملائكة وكل ما حدث من أمر القيامة لكان بلا شك يُؤْمِن بحقيقة دعوى المسيح وتكذيب إفتراء الرؤساء علي المخلص له المجد.

بطلان إفترائهم:

ومن ذلك قد ظهر عجزهم وخُذلانهم وحيرتهم، لأنهم لم يستطيعوا الوصول الي مأربهم بحجة يقبلها العقل أعظم مما ذكروا. وأي عاقل يُصدِق أن تلاميذه الذين هم صيادون من الجليل، يجسرون علي فتح قبر يحرسه الجنود الرومانيون.

وإذا فرضنا أنهم تجاسروا علي ذلك، فهل يكون لهم أقل رجاء للنجاح؟ إذ لا يتوقع قط أن يكون أولئك الحراس كلهم نياماً في وقتٍ واحدٍ مع علمهم أن قصاص من ينام وقت الحراسة يكون الموت.

وَمِمَّا يُبْطِل ويُسقِط حجتهم أيضاً إنه وإن صح أن الحراس كانوا نائمين كلهم، فمن أين عرفوا أن تلاميذه أو غيرهم هم الذين سرقوه. فليس لهم حينئذ سوي أن يقولوا نمنا ثم إستيقظنا فوجدنا القبر مفتوحاً خالياً من الميت.

وأنه لو كان بعضهم نياماً والبعض ساهرين كما هو مُشاهد في كل الحكومات والأنظمة المتبعة في قانون الحراسات. لَنَبَّه الساهرون النائمين ومنعوا التلاميذ من السرقة.

وأنه لو صّح أن الحراس ناموا وتركوا التلاميذ يسرقون الجسد ما كانوا تَرَكُوا الأكفان في القبر. بل حملوه بأكفانه. لأنه ما هو الداعي من نزع الأكفان عنه وأخذه عارياً. ويشيعون الخبر الكاذب بقيامته.

لماذا أن الرؤساء لا يغضبون علي الحراس ويسرعون الي بيلاطس ويشتكون عليهم

chastisement of the disciples for deceiving the government, disregarding the orders by breaking the seal, and stealing the body? Rather, we find the chief priests asking Pilate for the safety of the guards and not condemning them.

If Christ had not risen, what benefit would the disciples gain from stealing His body, and claiming His resurrection? They will only gain shame and reprimand from their own consciences, and suffer death from the governing authority.

The appearances of the Lord Jesus in the flesh after the Resurrection and the people to whom He appeared in diverse places:

1) To the women as they returned from the tomb (Mt 28:9).

2) To Mary Magdalene at the tomb (Mk 16:9; Jn 20:14).

3) To Peter (Lk 24:34; 1 Cor 15:5).

4) To two disciples as they traveled to Emmaus toward the evening (Lk 24:15; Mk 16:12).

5) To the apostles in the absence of Thomas, as they gathered in the Upper Room (Mk 16:14; Lk 24:36; Jn 20:19; 1 Cor 15:5).

In the aforementioned five instances, the appearances of the Savior were in Jerusalem and in Emmaus. This was during the first week of the Holy Resurrection.

6) To the apostles in Jerusalem in the presence of Thomas after the Lord's resurrection by eight days (Jn 20:24).

ويطلبـون قصاصهـم ويسـألونه القبـض عـلي التلاميـذ وعقابهـم عـلي خيانتهـم الحكومـة، وإسـتخفافهم بأوامرهـا بنزعهـم الختـم وسِرقهـم الجسـد، بـل نـري أن الرؤسـاء طلبـوا مـن بيلاطـس بـراءة الحـراس وعـدم ادانتهـم.

وإن لم يقـم المسـيح فـأي منفعـة للتلاميـذ مـن سرقـة جسـده وإدعائهـم بقيامتـه إذ ليـس لهـم مـن ذلـك سـوي العـار والتأنيـب مـن قِبـل الضمـير والعـذاب والمـوت مـن قِبـل السـلطة الحاكمـة.

ظهور الرب يسوع بالجسد بعد القيامة المجيدة والذين ظهر لهم في أماكن متعددة:

أولاً: ظهوره للنساءً وهن راجعات من القبر (مت ٩:٢٨).

ثانياً: ظهوره لمريم المجدلية عند القبر (مر٩:١٦)، (يو ١٤:٢٠).

ثالثاً: ظهوره لبطرس (لو ٣٤:٢٤)، (١ كو٥:١٥).

رابعـاً: ظهـوره لتلميذيـن وهـما منطلقـان إلي عمـواس نحـو المسـاء (لـو ١٥:٢٤)، (مـر ١٢:١٦).

خامسـاً: ظهـوره للرسـل في غيـاب تومـا وأيضـاً وهـم مجتمعـون (مـر ١٤:١٦)، (لـو ٣٦:٢٤)، (يـو ١٩:٢٠)، (١ كـو٥:١٥).

إن ظهـور المخلـص في هـذه المـرات الخمـس السـابقة كان في أورشـليم وفي عمـواس وكان ذلـك في الأسـبوع الأول لقيامتـه المقدسـة.

سادسـاً: ظهـوره للرسـل في حضـور تومـا بعـد قيامتـه بثمانيـة أيـام في أورشـليم (يـو ٢٤:٢٠).

7) To seven of the apostles on the shore of the Sea of Tiberius (Jn 21:1-2).

8) To the eleven apostles along with five hundred brethren on Mount Galilee (Mt 28:16-17; 1 Cor 15:6).

9) To James (1 Cor 15:7).

10) To the eleven in Jerusalem (Acts 1:3-8). After this appearance, He immediately ascended to heaven (Mk 16:19; Lk 24:50-51; Acts 1:9).

Benefits that we gained from the Glorious Resurrection

1) Conclusive proof of the validity of Christ's call. The resurrection is a divine heavenly testimony, believed by the apostles, who witnessed to it, and preached it all over the world. If the resurrection was not true, Christianity would have been in vain (1 Cor 15:14).

2) Verifying Christ's victory on humanity's final enemy: Death. All who have risen from the dead submitted to death once again, but Christ arose and death had no authority over Him.

3) Christ's resurrection is a token and foretelling of the general resurrection, because "Christ is risen from the dead, and has become the firstfruits of those who have fallen asleep" (1 Cor 15:20).

O, Son of God, who rose from the dead, triumphed over death, defeated hell, and conquered the abyss, raise us up from the slumber of sin, giving us victory over the body, the world, and the devil. O, Origin of Life and principle of resurrection, grant us the great joy, which You have granted to those in hell who believe in You. O, You who arose by the power of Your divinity, and trampled on death by Your death, grant us to live a spiritual life for You, and keep the death of sin from having dominion over us again. Amen.

سابعاً: ظهوره لسبعة من الرسل علي شاطىء بحر طبرية (يو ٢١: ١، ٢).

ثامناً: ظهوره للأحد عشر رسولا ولخمسمائة أخ علي جبل الجليل (مت ١٦:٢٨، ١٧)، (اكو ١٥:٦).

تاسعاً: ظهوره ليعقوب (اكو ١٥:٧).

عاشراً: ظهوره للأحد عشر في أورشليم (اع ١:٣ -٨)، وبعد هذا الظهور صعد حالاً إلي السماء (مر ١٦:١٩)، (لو ٥١،٢٤:٥٠)، (اع ١:٩).

الفوائد التي نلناها من القيامة المجيدة

اولاً: البرهان القاطع علي صحة دعوي المسيح. فالقيامة شهادة سمٰوية آلهية وإعتَقَدْها الرسل وشهدوا بها وكرزوا بها في كل المسكونة. ولولا صحة القيامة لكان الدين المسيحي باطلاً (١ كو١٥:١٤).

ثانياً: تحقيق إنتصار السيد المسيح علي عدو الإنسان الأخير أي الموت. فإن كل من قام من الأموات قبله خضع له ثانية، أما المسيح فقام ولَم يتسلط عليه الموت بعد.

ثالثاً: قيامة المسيح إنباء بالقيامة العامة وعُربون لها لأن السيد المسيح قد قام من بين الأموات وصار باكورة الراقدين (١ كو ١٥: ٢٠).

فيا إبن الله الذي قام من بين الأموات، وإنتصر علي الموت، وغلب الجحيم وقهر الهاوية، أقَمنا من نوم الخطية وإجعلنا أن ننتصر علي الجسد والعالم والشيطان. وَيَا عنصر الحياة ومبدأ القيامة أنعم علينا بالفرح العظيم الذي منحته للذين آمنوا بك في وسط الجحيم. وَيَا من قام بقوة لاهوته ووطئ الموت بموته أعطنا أن نحيا لك حياة روحية ولا يتسلط علينا موت الخطية مرة أخري. آمين.

ENDNOTES

1. According to Strong's "Bethany" 846, Bethany means "house of dates or house of misery."

2. Biblical references are taken from the NKJV, unless otherwise indicated.

3. Josephus, F., & Whiston, W. (1996). *The Works of Josephus : Complete and Unabridged*. Peabody: Hendrickson, 1751.

4. Josephus, F., & Whiston, W. (1996). *The Works of Josephus: Complete and Unabridged*. Peabody: Hendrickson. The War of the Jews or The History of the Destruction of Jerusalem, 1651.

5. Ibid, 1655.

6. Ibid, 1653.

7. Ibid.

8. Ibid, 1654.

9. Ibid, 1652.

10. Ibid, 1542.

11. Fifteen steps according to Josephus. Ibid, 1652.

12. Ibid.

13. Ibid, 1653.

14. Ibid, 1652.

15. Ibid, 1653.

16. Ibid, 1653.

17. Ibid, 1654.

18. Ibid, 1654.

19. Cf. Ibid, Bk 5, Ch 6; Bk 6, Ch 4.

20. Ibid, 1659.

21. Ibid, 1670.

22. Ibid, 1681.

23. Ibid, 1729.

24. Ibid, 1730.

25. Ibid.

26. Ibid.

27. Ibid, 1731.

28. Ibid.

29. Ibid, 1734.

30. Ibid, 1730.

31. Ibid, 1734–1735.

32. Cf. Ibid, 1735–1737.

33. Ibid, 1736.

34. Ibid, 1737.

35. Dix, G. (1945). *The shape of the Liturgy*. London: Dacre Press, 52.

36. The mention of stoning here refers to previous attempts of stoning Him, although not specified in Scripture as the anticipated method of death.

37. Tradition ascribes the title, "the thief on the right hand" to the penitent, Demas, though there is no mention of his exact position.

38. Cowper, Harris, *The Apocryphal Gospels and Other Documents Relating to the History of Christ*. London: Williams and Norgate, 1867, 221-222.

39. This sentence is found in the said book as: "Lentulus, president of the people of Jerusalem, to the Roman Senate and People: Greeting."

40. The writer has here evidently confounded Nazarenes with Nazirites.

www.ingramcontent.com/pod-product-compliance
Lightning Source LLC
Chambersburg PA
CBHW020949030426
42339CB00004B/10

9781939972194